Grace-
Energized
Women

To order a copy of this book write us at:
DISCOVER THE BOOK MINISTRIES
8500 N 128th E Avenue, Owasso, OK 74055-6242
or visit us online at:
discoverthebook.org

Grace-Energized Women
John S. Barnett

Müllerhaus Publishing Arts, Inc.
DBA Müllerhaus Legacy
5200 South Yale Ave, Penthouse | Tulsa, Oklahoma 74135
www.MullerhausLegacy.com

ISBN-13: 978-1-7328044-5-6
LCCN: 2019933108

© 2020 John S. Barnett
All rights reserved. Published 2020.
No part of this book may be reproduced, stored in a retrieval system, or transmitted in any form by an electronic, mechanical, photocopying, recording means, or otherwise, without prior written permission from the authors.

All Scripture quotations in this book, except those noted otherwise, are from the New King James Version of the Bible.

Scripture taken from the New King James Version®. Copyright © 1982 by Thomas Nelson. Used by permission. All rights reserved.

References marked NASB are scripture quotations taken from the New American Standard Bible® (NASB), Copyright © 1960, 1962, 1963, 1968, 1971, 1972, 1973, 1975, 1977, 1995 by The Lockman Foundation. Used by permission. www.Lockman.org

References marked NIV are scripture quotations taken from The Holy Bible, New International Version® NIV® Copyright © 1973 1978 1984 2011 by Biblica, Inc.™ Used by permission. All rights reserved worldwide.

Scripture quotations marked ESV are from the ESV® Bible (The Holy Bible, English Standard Version®), copyright © 2001 by Crossway Bibles, a publishing ministry of Good News Publishers. Used by permission. All rights reserved.

Cover and Interior Design by Kristin Stroup | Müllerhaus Legacy
Index by Nancy Kopper

Printed in Canada.

Grace-Energized Women

DR. JOHN S. BARNETT

Foreword by **Bonnie Marie Barnett**

müllerhaus
[LEGACY]

TULSA

Foreword
by Bonnie Marie Barnett

I can so clearly remember the day Joannie invited me into her life. John and I had only been married three months. We "honeymooned" driving across the country from New York to Los Angeles with all our earthly belongings packed into our little red Ford Escort, opening wedding cards as we drove to pay for the gas. We left all of our family and friends behind to become part of the ministry at Grace Community Church of the Valley serving under Pastor John MacArthur. On our first Sunday at the church of over 10,000 people, Joannie and her husband, Gorden, warmly welcomed us to their small group gathered around a table in the large gymnasium where their adult Sunday School class met.

We discovered that in all of greater Los Angeles, Joannie, her husband and family lived almost in the same neighborhood as we did. We lived at the bottom of the mountains in a stepsaver one bedroom apartment, and they lived up the side of the mountain in a lovely home with a yard and garden. Joannie was older than me and obviously in a different stage of life. Several of her children were grown and one teenager remained at home. I know Joannie had a very full life and yet she chose to open her heart and made room in her life for this needy young woman, me.

Joannie invited me to see Descanso Gardens (which later became a favorite place of respite and beauty for us in the midst of the hustle and bustle of L.A. life). She introduced me to the Bargain Box thrift store (where I still visit whenever I'm in L.A,).

Standing in our tiny living room apartment for the first time, Joannie noticed that our furniture consisted of a refurbished small sofa, an old desk and bookshelves John had built out of boards and cement blocks. Joannie kindly offered that her friend was looking for a new home for a living room chair and wondered if we might like it. The next time she visited, Joannie brought the lovely blue velvet covered chair and placed it next to our homemade bookshelf.

At Thanksgiving Joannie invited John and me to join their family for Thanksgiving dinner in their home. I learned how to make perfectly smooth turkey gravy watching Joannie at her stove. You see, my Mom died of cancer 14 days after John and I were engaged and I had never taken a big interest in any part of homemaking.

I didn't become a believer in Jesus Christ until I was 21. Before that, Bonnie lived for Bonnie. My life revolved around me. By the time I was 21, I had tried about everything the world had to offer and always came up empty, shattered and hopeless. One night alone in a terrific blizzard, I reached the bottom. It was then I pleaded with God to show me the truth about life and eternity.

A faithful Gideon had given a green New Testament to my brother. Opening the crisp pages to Matthew, I began reading the greatest truth ever told. I read all night, Matthew, Mark, Luke and John. Never had I known of such great love and sacrifice. Jesus Christ, the Son of God, became a man and took upon Him the penalty for all my sin.

> "For God so loved the world that He gave His only Son, that whoever believes in Him should not perish but have eternal life. For God did not send His Son into the world to condemn the world, but in order that the world might be saved through Him."
> John 3:16-17 (ESV)

As my heart broke in repentance, I turned from my evil ways that night and received forgiveness for all my sin and new life in my Lord and Savior,

Jesus Christ. The Son of God set me free and became the King of my heart. My life belongs to Him and Him alone. At once, God began leading, providing, and preparing me to serve Him. Five years later after graduating from a Christian university, I met and married John Barnett. But that story would fill another book!

Now, as a new bride far from home, I watched everything Joannie did and listened as she showered love and respect upon her children and husband. From her gentle spirit, kind words, joyful laugh and patient love, I saw Jesus living in her and through her. Before Christmas, Joannie invited me into her home to make homemade Christmas gifts. We drew our own designs and stenciled dish towels to give to loved ones.

I learned more than I can put into words from Joannie coming alongside me as a Titus 2 older woman. I learned so much more than how to make gravy or a stencil. Joannie modeled for me how to invest my life in eternal matters, in what would last forever, first in knowing and growing in my love for my Savior Jesus Christ, and secondly in lovingly caring for and investing in my husband, children and others.

One of my favorite sermons I have heard John preach is about the dash. It's the dash between the date of our birth and the date of our death. That little dash stands in the place representing everything we lived for on this earth. If you look in the Scriptures, you'll notice God often summarizes an entire life by "he died and he did evil in the sight of the Lord" or "he died and did what was right in the sight of the Lord". That's what this book is about, learning to live every day by the grace of God and realizing we live it in His sight. God cares about what is in our heart and how we apply our hearts to live our days and years for Him alone obeying and trusting in His everlasting Word.

I have been married and a pastor's wife for over three decades now. It has been my highest privilege to learn from John's profound teaching of God's Word and to invest my life serving alongside His gifted servant. I am also thankful for the river of older godly women God placed in the pathway of my life. I have learned something from each one. I thank God for the younger women, including my own daughters, whom God continues to place in my life and pray I may be an example to them.

It has been my joy to share the beautiful truths found in Titus 2 with women all around the world — newlyweds, students, refugees, missionaries and pastors' wives. I invite you to read carefully, understanding the treasure found in God's Word and God's high calling for every woman, young and old. I pray you will understand God's Word more clearly and invest your moments and your days in what God says will last for eternity, that one day you may hear Him say to you, *"Well done, good and faithful servant... enter into the joy of your Lord."*

Bonnie Barnett
Colossians 3:16-17

Energized by Grace | *1*

The church that met two thousand years ago was very simple. There were no church buildings, so homes or public places were used. There were no written materials other than God's word. No books, no tapes, no videos, no projectors, no parking lots, no auditoriums. Just people indwelt by God's Spirit and His Word.

When first-century believers met, they were given very simple marching orders. A mission. And two thousand years later, regardless of language, culture, time period, social issues, family values, laws and rights and protests, and two millennia of opinions and teachings, that mission has not changed. To be a twenty-first-century woman of grace, the mission is simple. Please God.

THE GRACE OF GOD THAT BRINGS SALVATION

When you woke up this morning and peered into the mirror, did you say to yourself, "My highest desire today is to let God change me from the inside out?" Is it your top goal to love God with all your heart and live every moment for Him? Titus 2 tells us how you can . . . by His grace!

As we look deeply into the mirror of God's Word we will discover what God meant by: reverent in behavior, not slanderers, not given to much wine, teachers of good things, that they admonish, to love their husbands, to love their children, to be discreet, chaste, homemakers, good, and obedient to their own husbands.

God's grace teaches us how to live for Him every day. "For the grace of God that brings salvation has appeared to all men, teaching us that, denying ungodliness and worldly lusts, we should live soberly, righteously, and godly in this present age, looking for the blessed hope and glorious appearing of our great God and Savior Jesus Christ, who gave Himself for us, that He might redeem us from every lawless deed and purify for Himself His own special people, zealous for good works."[1]

Every day, we can live obediently, pleasing to God, or disobediently, displeasing to God. What difference does it make? Amazingly, neither obedience nor disobedience changes God's love. There is nothing that I can do to make God love me more, or make Him love me less. Sin does not make God's love meter go up and down. He's not like us. His love never fails and never changes. My sin or my obedience doesn't change that.

But our choices do determine our eternal reward.[2] And Jesus adds to that our eternal status in heaven.[3] Really. The Scriptures tell us that those who live for God in obedience, by their example in ministry, and influence others to follow God will forever display God's glory. Daniel says that those that turn many to righteousness will shine like the stars forever.[4] But those who don't won't.

Paul adds that there are some who will suffer loss when the Judgment Seat comes and the rewards are given.[5] And John goes even further and says there are those who, because of their unwillingness to respond to the Word, will be ashamed before the Lord at His coming.[6]

The All-Consuming Mission for Every Woman of Grace

The Apostle Paul reduced the Christian life down to two words. The man who wrote more of the New Testament than anyone, who preached

---

1   Titus 2:11–14
2   2 Corinthians 5:10
3   Matthew 25:14–30
4   Daniel 12:3
5   1 Corinthians 3:15
6   1 John 2:28

more sermons and mentored more pastors and planted more churches distilled down everything in the Christian life to only two simple words: please God.

"Finally then, brethren, we urge and exhort in the Lord Jesus that you should abound more and more, just as you received from us how you ought to walk and how to," and there it is, "please God."[7]

But when Paul summed up the Christian life in 1 Thessalonians 4:1, he didn't just say to the Thessalonians, "please God." He said, "We urge you." That is a continuous active indicative. That means he was continuously, actively urging and exhorting. He was constantly urging the believers at Thessalonica to stay on track with their mission in life, and that mission is to please God. Everything else falls under those two words.

Pleasing God is not an accident. It doesn't just happen. The word Paul used doesn't just mean "to please." It means "to strive to please, to accommodate oneself to the desires and interests of another."

Paul continuously reminded them that they had a mission every day of life, and that was to please God. Think about today, and each new day, as launching out on a mission to please God in everything throughout the day and night, everywhere you are, and in everything you do. That was the mission that marked the New Testament saints.

This mission is accomplished only by grace, and God assures us that His grace gives us the strength. God's grace energizes us to do all that pleases Him. "So now brethren," Paul says, "I commend you to God and to the word of His grace, which is able to build you up and give you an inheritance among all those who are sanctified."[8]

The message of grace, that God has already done everything necessary for salvation, seems impossible. Paul even says it sounds foolish.[9] But God's amazing grace has the power to save, and it is what gives us the complete power to please God in everything we do.

But it's not automatic. Salvation was a gift by the grace of God, but to live a life pleasing to God requires something of me. And God, in His grace, has spelled out for us exactly what is required of us to live a life of godliness.

7   1 Thessalonians 4:1
8   Acts 20:32
9   1 Corinthians 1:18

Paul reduced the Christian life to, in the first century, getting up every day as a slave or as a businessman or as an army officer and deciding by His grace, "I'm going to please God." It's not just an attitude. It's simple choices. And Titus 2 has a list of twelve clearly defined choices we can make to either please God, and intentionally, systematically, incrementally, inch-by-inch have those twelve things showing up in our life, or we can say, "I don't really care. Doesn't really matter to me."

The Warning Lights of a Life Not Energized by Grace

The twelve qualities of Titus 2 are not God's twelve suggestions for women of grace. These are not twelve personality traits of some Christians. These are twelve commands, twelve expectations, twelve virtues that God is looking for in every woman.

Every car is equipped with warning lights of various shapes, colors and locations. Sometimes when a light comes on, we are not quite sure what it indicates and we quickly consult the Owner's Manual. Likewise, warning lights of our lives should motivate us to consult the manual of our lives—God's Word.

What are the warning lights of a woman who is not energized by grace? If you are not following God's plan for your life as a woman, then no matter how good your life looks on the outside, one or more of these warning lights will indicate a problem.

First, without a grace-energized foundation of God's word, this woman will become irresponsible. She doesn't know what God wants, and so she doesn't fulfill her responsibilities. She never seems to be able to get around to doing what God wants her to do. She just aimlessly wanders through life.

Second, without the grace-energized power of God's word, she will become an emotionally detached wife. This woman may be recognized as one of the most stable and even-tempered women in her community. She may be frequently asked to serve on boards and numerous ministries because of her organized mind and methodical way of decision making. However, in her home, she is as detached and emotionally unavailable as a woman can be.

Third, without grace-energized obedience to God's Word, she will become a dictatorial wife. Remember, we are not supposed to just hear God's Word. We're supposed to do it. This woman's idea of marriage is that nothing happens without her approval. If her husband dares to question her, she resorts to manipulation or even intimidating tactics.

Fourth, without the grace-energized pattern of God's word, she becomes a workaholic wife. This woman never quits working, physically or emotionally. She sprays her family with her frustrations. That's not the way that God designed life. When everything is under His control, then nothing is out of control.

Fifth, without the grace-energized nurture of God's Word, she'll become a spiritually apathetic wife. This woman is a believer and a church attendee but beyond that, she's generally unresponsive to spiritual matters.

A Life Powered by Grace

This side of heaven, we'll never be perfect, we'll never be sinless, we'll never live up to all God wants us to be, but all who are saved are progressively being sanctified. That's grace-energized living.

When God says that grace-energized women are to love their husbands, it means by nature, they don't. And when it says we are to love our children, it means that by nature, humanly, we wouldn't. And when it says that we should be kind, it means that we're not. So we're faced with God's standard, and where we are. And if this is not the direction your life is pointing, you can, right now, have a change of mind that leads to a change in behavior. It's called repentance.

Paul tells Titus in Titus 2:11 that the grace of God is our teacher, and it teaches us in Philippians 2:12, "work out your own salvation with fear and trembling." Take this salvation that you already have—that was all God, nothing of yourself, completely by grace—take that salvation that's already yours, and go to work.

The word is *energea*—like "energy" or "energize." It means "to work fervently at." Throughout the New Testament, Paul describes the Christian life as a struggle, like an athlete straining every muscle toward one goal. Whether it's Peter's list of the seven characteristics of the godly life from

2 Peter 1, or Paul's list of the fruit of the Spirit in Galatians, those qualities grow out of a vital relationship with Jesus Christ. But as Peter and Paul clarify, we don't just sit there and have them happen. Peter clearly says, "make every effort" and as Paul says, "work out" these qualities in your life.

It's not passive. It's not automatic. It's a struggle. Grace-energized living does not come naturally. But when Paul says, "work out your own salvation" in Philippians 2:12, look how he follows that up: "For it is God who" *energea*, "works in you both to will and to do for His good pleasure."

Did you notice the goal we're straining for? His "good pleasure," to "please God"? But God didn't just save us by His grace, leave us everything we need for life and godliness and let us go. No. He is actively, presently working in us. *Energea*. His grace energizes us.

It's like when you go to the dentist. The dentist stands over you with the light shining in your face, and he asks for a tool, and the dental assistant places in his hand exactly what he needs to accomplish what needs to be done. As we look at Titus 2, Jesus Christ is the One who wants to accomplish in us every one of these twelve qualities. And as we say, "yes, that's what I want," and put our hand out, he places into our hands and our hearts everything that we need.

When we take specific, earnest, even agonizing steps in our life toward what God wants, do you know what we find? The instant we do that, the instant we by faith say, "God, Your virtue, Your quality, Your discipline that You want in my life, that is what I want. And I see where I am and I see where You want me to be, and I want to go that way," the instant we do that, we find that God gives us the strength, the power of His Spirit, to accomplish that. Once we say "yes," He gives us the help to take the earnest active steps to obey Him, and each step we take, we find amazingly that He gives us the spiritual power and strength to be changing areas of our life that have stubbornly stayed the same for so long.

Titus 2:3–5 are our marching orders. There is no clearer pattern for a godly woman in all of God's Word than these twelve character qualities recorded in these verses. This is what God desires, explains, and expects from obedient and godly women. If you're looking for a passage to study in depth that can change your life, here it is. If you want a special passage to memorize and meditate on that can transform your thinking and life's direction, this is it. And if you want to go through life confident you are doing exactly what God wants you to do each day, Titus 2:3-5 are your words to live by. I invite you to come along to study God's rich word as we look deeply into Titus 2. Let us make this our prayer today and every day that we live by grace pleasing to God.

Lord, let Your grace energize us daily as we seek to do Your will. Let it infuse us with Your power to say no to sin and yes to You. May the grace of God, which came to us and brought us Your salvation, also teach us, enable us to obey, and make us zealous for the good works You have prepared for us to do. And so let us shine like lights in a dark world, with marriages and families that draw the world to Your Light, Lord Jesus, so that they want what we have, and we share it with them. This we pray in Your name, amen.

Respond to Truth

If you were to sum up your mission for today, what would it be? If it were "please God," what choices might you have made differently?

How would you describe grace? How else does God describe grace (Acts 20:32; Romans 1:5, 6:12–14; 1 Corinthians 15:10; 2 Corinthians 9:8; Titus 2:11–14; 2 Peter 3:18)?

How closely does God's Word, written thousands of years ago, match His desires and expectations for today (1 Samuel 15:29; Psalm 55:19, 102:25–27, 119:89; Matthew 5:18; Luke 16:17)?

Knowing God wants to energize you by His grace, if you were to line up and measure yourself against the teaching of Titus 2, in which areas are you growing?

Holy Lives in an Unholy World | 2

REPRESENTATIVES OF GOD

One of the most beloved chapters for women, wives, and mothers is that venerable old chapter 31 of Proverbs. There we see in the Old Testament that incredible woman of virtue whose pricelessness is beyond rubies. She is the woman of excellence, the mother of mothers, and the wife that excels them all.

For centuries, the Proverbs 31 woman has been extolled and held forth as a model for all, but when that passage is read, often on Mother's Day, many women sit a little lower in their seats as the Proverbs 31 woman seems to never sleep, never tire, never fail, and seems to be just plain perfect.

As much as we love that passage, it never claims to be God's command for every woman. Proverbs 31 was never meant to be a one-size-fits-all for women of all ages, and God does not expect every godly woman to stay up all night, to sew clothes for every member of her household, to be a gourmet chef, to sell her wares on the side, and to be an expert on every domestic topic including the buying and selling of land. It's a picture of what one virtuous woman's life looked like.

But on the opposite end of the spectrum from the inspirational Proverbs 31 woman is the God-designed Titus 2 woman of grace. This is

God's expectation for every woman, and unlike the often-unattainable standard set in Proverbs 31, Titus 2 is something every woman can live by.

"The older women likewise, that they be reverent in behavior, not slanderers, not given to much wine, teachers of good things—that they admonish the young women to love their husbands, to love their children, to be discreet, chaste, homemakers, good, obedient to their own husbands, that the word of God may not be blasphemed."[1]

At the very top of the list, Paul draws a word from the Roman world that's so distant to us today: "reverent." To understand this word, we need to first remember who he was writing to. The book of Titus was written primarily to a group of people way out in the Mediterranean Sea on an island called Crete. It's still there today, and that's who Paul was writing to.

But secondly and wonderfully, he was also writing to us, to all of Christ's Church. This book wasn't written solely to them. But it was written directly to them. And what they would have understood immediately when they read this letter is what Paul meant when he used the word "reverent."

This was the word used in the ancient world to describe the behavior of a priest. Remember, all of the people first receiving this letter used to be pagans, and they worshiped pagan gods before they were gloriously saved by Jesus Christ.

In the ancient world, temples were always built outside of town. I didn't realize this until the last trip we took to the Middle East, and we were walking around Ephesus and I saw this marble walkway leading out of town. So I asked our guide what that was, and he said, "Oh, that's the sacred way." These are all over Asia Minor. First you had to bathe and change your clothes, and then this priest or priestess would lead you out of the city on this sacred way to the temple. If you wanted access to the gods, you had to follow this priest.

There were several things about this priest or priestess that were immediately recognizable. They would walk in this slow, reverent way, and everyone who followed them had to walk the same way they did. When you saw them in town, you'd recognize them immediately by the clothes they wore. Everything about them told you they were a representative of a god.

---

1   Titus 2:3–5

So that's the word Paul uses. "The older women likewise, that they be" exactly like this pagan priestess who led people up the sacred way into the presence of their god.

Do you know what the most impressive feature of any town was? Their temple. Especially Ephesus. The golden temple to Artemis was one of the wonders of the ancient world. It was ten stories high, the size of a city block, and covered with pure gold. If you came into Ephesus, you wouldn't notice the bustling harbor or the marketplace teeming with people buying and selling their wares. You would be practically blinded looking up at that huge, golden temple.

So, everyone, no matter what city they lived in in the Roman Empire, would have immediately pictured all this when Paul said "reverent." The gods, the temples, the priests, and they would have gone back to what they were taught, that God was so much greater than any of that. And He had the power to completely change their lives, to bring them out of all that. And this God, who has the ultimate power, who is greater than anything, wants godly older women to be His representatives. He wants them to be immediately recognizable, by the way they walk, by the way they talk, by the way they dress, and that they lead others into the presence, not of an idol made of wood or stone, but into the presence of the true and living God.

Notice what Titus 2:3 says, that the older women are to be reverent "in behavior." In other words, this priest-like attitude spreads through their whole life. It permeates everything. It's the Greek word *semnos*, and it means august, venerable, honorable, or in the context of the local church, a woman who lives in such a godly way she can be emulated and venerated for her character.

The Church is to be filled with women who are models of Christ. There is no higher usefulness than that, and Paul calls all of us in Christ's Church to the same high calling. The same basic word is used for deacons,[2] for older men,[3] and it extends to the life of every believer. First Timothy 2:2–4 says, "That we may lead a quiet and peaceable life in all godliness and," there's

---

2   1 Timothy 3:8
3   Titus 2:2

that word again, "reverence." Why? "For this is good and acceptable in the sight of God our Savior, who desires all men to be saved and to come to the knowledge of the truth."

Paul uses the same idea in 1 Timothy 3:11 when he says women are to be "dignified," in the NASB, or as the NIV says, "worthy of respect." This is talking about a behavior that is beautifully desired to be emulated. Someone who is revered. That makes people say, "I want to follow the Lord like she does."

If God could reduce your priorities down to a "to do the most vital thing first" list, what would rise to the top? What is the most important thing for every woman to strive for? The first priority for every godly woman is to be priest-like in her behavior. To be a representative of God. Godly older women are to lead people, with their behavior, into the presence of God. The unsaved to a knowledge of the truth. The younger women in the church to a lifestyle that pleases God. By the way she walks, by the way she talks, by the way she dresses and everything else, she represents God, and when people see her, they say, "I want to follow the Lord like she does." That's the highest priority of a woman of grace.

THE DAILY CHOICES OF A REVERENT WOMAN

She Presents Her Body a Living Sacrifice

The Titus 2 woman makes three daily choices to be reverent in her behavior, and she, first of all, chooses to take Romans 12:1–2 seriously. She chooses to surrender daily to the Lord.

"I beseech you therefore, brethren, by the mercies of God, that you present your bodies a living sacrifice, holy, acceptable to God, which is your reasonable service."

In a simple, practical way, her body is a living sacrifice. That means her goals, her desires, her plans, her aspirations, her career, her drive, her priorities are not her own. She sacrifices what she wants for what God wants in each area of her life.

Because she chooses to surrender daily to the Lord, she is not conformed to the world (Romans 12:2). Conformity to the world is not an active choice. Everyone becomes slowly conformed to the world if they do not, like this woman of reverence, make a daily choice not to be squeezed into the world's mold. She asks herself, does it please God that I go to this place, that I do this, that I watch that, that I listen to this? And if not, she refuses to let the pressure of the world and what's popular and what's acceptable and what's expected squeeze her into what does not please God.

How? How do we resist the squeezing, conforming pressure of the world that is constantly there? By the transforming power of a renewed mind. Look at the end of Romans 12:2. The woman who presents her body a living sacrifice by surrendering daily to the Lord, who is not conformed to the world because she is constantly running her every decision by the God she serves, is renewed daily in the spirit of her mind. She fills her mind with what is profitable (Timothy 3:16), with what is true (Philippians 4:8), and with what encourages reverent behavior.

She Behaves as a Walking, Talking Temple of God

The godly woman of reverence, number two, reminds herself daily that she is God's temple. Did you know that we are living, breathing, walking, talking temples of the God of the universe? And as a representative of God, this godly woman constantly reminds herself that she is the temple of God.

The temples of the ancient world were magnificent, monuments of man's achievements, covered with gold and everything else. But if you visit Asia Minor, modern-day Turkey, you would find nothing left of those temples but ruins. The believers in the first century, and we, have been given the incredible privilege and responsibility to be the imperishable, living temples of the true and living God.

It makes me think of every time my wife was pregnant with any one of our eight children. She would act differently. She didn't want to bump into stuff. I remember when she was expecting our sixth child, I took her to Mammoth Cave. You enter Mammoth Cave by going down a stairway of what seemed like hundreds of steps. And all the people were so nice, and my wife was in her thirty-eighth week, so they all said, "Oh, you go to the front of the line." So my wife was at the front of the line, clunking down these hundreds of steps with me helping her so she didn't fall, and with two hundred people behind us.

And we get to the bottom, and the doorway to the Mammoth Cave is only so wide. So my wife tried to fit this way, and tried to fit that way, and finally she just had to squeeze through because there were two hundred people behind us. But you act differently when you're carrying something of that magnitude, like a little life. You have to be careful what you do and where you go and what you're exposed to.

Do you know that many believers are carrying around the precious Spirit of God inside them and they're bumping into things, breathing toxic fumes, drinking and smoking and eating a steady diet of what's harmful and offensive to the Holy Spirit inside them? "Or do you not know," Paul says, "that your body is the temple of the Holy Spirit who is in you, whom you have from God, and you are not your own? For you were bought with a price; therefore glorify God in your body and in your spirit, which are God's."[4]

You know what God says? Your body is the mobile temple of the Holy Spirit. Therefore glorify God as your body walks around and your spirit responds to people, because both of them belong to God. The second choice God asks for is to remind ourselves daily that we are His temple, and we act differently because we're carrying around something very precious. It alters how I eat, what I expose myself to, how I behave, and how I conduct myself.

But do you know what else a temple is? It's not just the place for God to dwell; it's the place where you go to meet God. Even the ancient temples, even though the gods were false, they were the places where you would go to meet your god. But you and I are the representatives of Christ. We are His temple. He lives in us. He lives through us. And people see Christ in our actions and in our behavior, and they are drawn to Him. That's why it says in Titus that the pagans will be ashamed and unable to speak evil of us because they see such consistency.

When we live as temples of Christ, the place for the world to come and meet God, they will realize that we know how to live and we know how to die and they don't. And they'll want that. They don't have hope, they don't

---

4   1 Corinthians 6:19–20

have joy, they don't have peace, they don't have harmony in their homes, and they don't have peace in their minds, but we do. That's what living like God's temple does.

She Lives Out Her High Calling as God's Priest

The godly woman of reverence, thirdly, chooses to follow her calling. Ephesians 2:10, "For we are His workmanship, created in Christ Jesus for good works, which God prepared beforehand that we should walk in them."

Ephesians 4:1, "I, therefore, the prisoner of the Lord, beseech you to walk in a manner worthy of the calling with which you were called." How do we do that? How do we follow this high calling from God?

The highest calling is not what everyone thinks you should do, or even what your parents or friends say. It's what God designed you to do. You want to know what good works God has prepared for you to do? They're not a mystery. It's not like we walk around asking, "What good works do You want me to do today, Lord?"

He's written them out. Titus 2 is one of those places. Twelve good works that God has prepared beforehand for every godly woman to walk in, as His workmanship, His masterpiece.

She Learns the Secret of Putting Off and Putting On

God's will for our lives is not a secret. It's not a mystery. What He wants us to know, He writes down in His Word. If you want to be a representative of God, read the instruction manual, and learn the secret of putting off and putting on.

God's will, not just for the older women who by their reverent behavior are examples to the rest, but for every believer, is to cultivate holy habits. It is not an easy thing to, every day, every moment, continuously be making conscious choices to please God, asking constantly what pleases Him, consulting Him on everything. But habits are what we do when we don't make a conscious choice. Habits are the default settings of our soul. When we don't consciously plan our behavior, we are taken over by habit.

It is easier to operate by habit than to purposefully choose each act. Therefore perhaps the most powerful part of our lives is that box of mental auto-choices we call our habits. And women who present themselves a living sacrifice, who behave as a walking, talking temple of God, and who live out their high calling do so because they have formed habits that honor God.

Ephesians 4:22–24 contain three holy habits that lead to sacrificed living, and priest-like behavior, and acting like God's temple. These three habits are the secret of putting off and putting on.

THE HABIT OF GRACE-PROMPTED SHEDDING

Have you ever wondered how believers like those at Crete, or those at Ephesus, who were just as pagan, just as godless, just as steeped in the Greco-Roman culture of debauchery and indulgence in every lust of the flesh as the people on Crete, how those people became the kind of men and women who led people into the presence of God?

"Put off, concerning your former conduct, the old man which grows corrupt according to the deceitful lusts."[5]

Paul spoke of the old man, the old self, like a set of clothes that we've become so used to wearing we don't even think about it anymore. But we have been changed. We have been redeemed and justified, and we are being sanctified. And everything that belongs to the old man, the habits, the desires, the goals, the lifestyle that used to characterize us, before Christ, is supposed to be shed like an old garment. David puts it this way: "It shall not cling to me."[6]

As long as we live in a world of sin, we will not somehow stop sinning. But what Paul says, and what David says, is that as soon as we sin, as soon as that old self pops up again, we scrape it off. It will not cling to me.

I used to live on a horse farm, and when you live on a horse farm, stuff clings to you. You can't go walking through the field without picking up, on your boots, stuff that you do not want in your house. So you don't go in the front door. You go into the garage and you carefully scrape off everything that you picked up walking through the field. And that's the habit David learned. That's the habit Paul taught. And that's the habit Ephesus caught in Acts 19.

---

5   Ephesians 4:22
6   Psalm 101:3

In Acts 19, we see Ephesus as it was before it became the Christian book-publishing center of the ancient world. Before it became a church 50,000 strong, known for their works, their labor, their faith. Before they were known for their love of Christ. And Paul taught them to scrape off the old man. So what did they do with that teaching?

"And many who had believed came confessing and telling their deeds. Also, many of those who had practiced magic brought their books together and burned them in the sight of all. And they counted up the value of them, and it totaled fifty thousand pieces of silver. So the word of God grew mightily and prevailed."[7]

These were expensive books. They were beautifully illustrated, practically pieces of art, but the believers at Ephesus, when they learned how Satan worked, wanted to get rid of anything from their old lives that didn't please God, and they scraped it all out of their houses, brought it out on the front lawn, and burned it.

That's grace-prompted shedding. It's like that TV show, *What Not to Wear*. When you see in God's Word what He says you should not be wearing as a representative of His, you don't fold it back up and put it in a drawer. You take it out on the front lawn and, like the Ephesians, set it on fire.

The result of that consecrated life is found in Acts 19:20. "So the word of the Lord grew mightily and prevailed." And that is also how we know what to put off and to put on, which brings us to the second holy habit.

The Habit of Grace-Prompted Thinking

"Be renewed in the spirit of your mind."[8]

Do you remember what a woman who takes Romans 12:1–2 seriously does? She presents her body a living sacrifice, she refuses to be conformed to the world, and she renews her mind. How? How is our mind renewed?

Did you know that the habits you form, the thoughts you think, the actions you repeat, form ruts in your mind? Your brain is chemically altered, like grooves on a record, and those paths are formed every time you go over and over the same patterns of behavior or patterns of thinking.

7   Acts 19:18–20
8   Ephesians 4:23

If you believe right, you behave right. Right behavior, the secret of putting off and putting on, begins with a renewed mind. With repaving over the ruts, smoothing over the grooves in your mind with the Word of God.

The word Paul used for "reverent" in Titus 2 is found in another form in one of his other epistles. You probably know this one: "Finally, brethren, whatever things are true, whatever things are," and there's that word, "noble."[9] Just another form of the word "reverent." In the list of what things we are to think, Paul says we are to think on what leads to noble or reverent or priest-like behavior.

Paul is reminding the early believers that what they thought about and allowed to stay on their minds is what they would become. When you think about noble things, about reverent, godly things, it directs your whole life toward becoming that. And a Titus 2 woman knows whatever she reads, whatever she listens to, whatever she watches, whatever she allows to stay on her mind, that's what she'll become.

The other day I was driving past a cornfield, and this giant harvester was going down the rows of corn and knocking down the stalks and making all this noise. I actually stopped the car to see the stream that was coming out the back. It looked like gold. And I thought, whatever's coming in the front as it's knocking down and chewing up, that's what's coming out the back. And whatever comes in the front of our life, through our eyes, our ears, into our minds, that's what's going to come out of our lives.

Proverbs 23:7 says, "For as he thinks in his heart, so is he." That means if you allow television, movies, music, gaming, or any other media to stimulate your flesh, to feed your mind with lying and profanity and illegitimate sexual things and gossip and occult images and so much more, then your mind will slowly depart from what the Bible says is noble and dignified and worthy of respect. And soon, your actions will follow your mind, and you will not be acting reverent in your behavior.

If your corn harvester grinds up and processes all those bad things and every so often there's this bunch of wonderful truth from God's Word that just gets mixed in there, it dilutes God's Word, and it doesn't come out in the life. You have to change the combine intake to change the outflow

9   Philippians 4:8

of the life. If you want to have a reverent life, think about, Philippians 4:8, what is true, and what is lovely, and whatever lines up with God's Word and is of good repute and noble and dignified. And soon after, your actions will follow.

What you are on the outside, reverent or not, started a long time ago on the inside. The key to reverent behavior is found in the diet a godly mind desires and hungers after. Every child of God who wants to live a holy, reverent life in the midst of an unholy world has to start watching what their mind feeds on. You are what you eat; garbage coming in is defilement coming out. And garbage avoided is defilement avoided. You want to avoid something bad coming out of your life? Don't process it in on the front end.

The Habit of Grace-Prompted Wearing

"Put on the new man which was created according to God, in true righteousness and holiness."[10]

The secret of putting off and putting on centers around grace-prompted thinking. When your mind is renewed, your life is consecrated, and what doesn't please God is systematically scraped off, thrown out, set on fire if necessary. But it doesn't end there. Women of grace, prompted by grace and energized by grace, begin to put on what is pleasing to God. Do you want to be beautiful in God's sight? Put on what He says is beautiful to Him.

When God lists for us in Titus 2 the qualities He's looking for in a godly woman, what He's giving us is a dress code. This is pleasing in His sight. This is beautiful to Him. This is what He wants to see His godly women putting on every day. And the first one is reverence.

Reverence is the quality that enables all the others. See, you can't be a woman whose speech is under control if you're not presenting yourself as a living sacrifice to God. You won't become a woman whose appetites are disciplined if you don't remind yourself that you are a temple of the Holy Spirit who lives inside you. You won't be able to model and teach younger women if you're not living out your high calling as a priest of God. Every item on that list is a matter of putting off an old behavior and allowing God to renew your mind so that you can put on a new behavior. That's why

10 Ephesians 4:24

"reverent in behavior" is first, because a life that has been dedicated to God is the first step to a life that is pleasing to God in every other way.

If you want to be a woman who is filled to the full and overflowing with the grace of God, then this is where you start. Will you make that your commitment today?

Father, thank You that we don't have to have any doubts about how You want us to live. Rivet all of our hearts to a lifestyle of representing You. May we be known, wherever we are, every day of our lives, as Your representatives. At work, at school, at home, in the lives of our children, in the lives of our family, and in our personal lives, let us represent You as Your priests. As Your living temple. Fully surrendered to You. We put out our hands of faith to You. Put into our hearts what we need to accomplish what You desire from us today. In Jesus' name we pray, amen.

Respond to Truth

If those around you started following the Lord like you do, would you be leading people into the presence of God, or away from Him? Would someone watching your life say, "I want to follow the Lord like she does"?

What parts of your behavior don't immediately identify you as God's representative? How can you, in a simple, practical way, surrender those areas to God's complete control today?

What parts of your mental diet might be offensive or harmful to the Holy Spirit dwelling inside you? What toxic influences are you allowing yourself to be exposed to? How would the temple of the living God respond to those things?

How are you renewing your mind through God's Word? If this is what God's first priority for women of grace centers around, how can you take practical steps to making this your first priority as well?

What one item of spiritual clothing can you put on to be beautiful for Jesus Christ today (Ephesians 4:25–32; Colossians 3:12–17)? How?

3 | Speaking Gracefully in a Graceless World

THE GREAT ACCUSER

Right now, Satan is roaming the earth trying to destroy God's plan. He is, without exception, the highest, greatest, most powerful created being in the universe. And he is very focused in his method of attack.

Satan is revealed in God's Word by many names, and each of those names also reveals one of his methods of attack against God and His people. He's called Lucifer, the angelic being, the ministering spirit. By the way, he's not wearing red pajamas and carrying a pitchfork. He was one of those burning, powerful, angelic beings that were always in the presence of God. You can read about it in Isaiah 14 and Ezekiel 28. He used to be the "covering cherub," wings outstretched like one of those parabolic reflectors that a photographer might use to increase the flash, and his job was to reflect back the glory of God as he hovered over the throne.

But somewhere along the way, Lucifer started enjoying the glory, and in his pride, he wanted to be like God. That shows you the inspiration of Scripture. He didn't want to be greater or more powerful than God. He didn't want to be better than God. He just wanted to be equal, because nothing could possibly be better, more powerful, or greater than God. He just wanted to be *like* God, to share in His power. And because of that, he fell.

Secondly, he's called Satan, which means "the Adversary." He's always been the enemy, the adversary, of God's plan and God's people.

He's also called the serpent from of old, who deceived Eve in the Garden of Eden. He's the one who introduced sin into the world, and through the deception of Eve, with Adam following her in that deception, sin spread throughout the world.

He's also the Dragon in Revelation 12, relentlessly seeking to destroy Israel, the chosen people of God. From God's first words to Abraham, God promised an eternal covenant with Abraham's descendants, and throughout history, we can watch God's plan unfolding if we keep our eye on the Jewish people. But Satan knows enough about the Bible to relentlessly try to destroy God's chosen nation.

He's also known as the Deceiver, the one who enslaves the minds and hearts of the whole world. First John 5 says the whole world is in the lap of the evil one.

He's also the murderer from the beginning, showing up wherever mankind shows a desire to steal and kill and destroy. Did you know his element, his medium in which he operates, is stealing, killing, and destroying? And more and more of our media and entertainment centers on the things Satan thrives on.

He's also, 1 Peter 5 says, the roaring lion that seeks to devour unsuspecting believers. But none of those is his most dangerous name.

Titus 2:3 contains the most dangerous name of Satan, and therefore his most damaging method of attacking Christ's Church. The most constant, the most repeated, the most widely occurring damage in the Church does not come from the destroying Dragon or the deceiver of the world. It comes from the name in Titus 2:3. That name is the Devil, or *diabolous*, or, literally, "the Slandering Accuser."

The Bible repeatedly shows Satan accusing God's people before God's throne. We see it in the book of Job, and it shows up again in Revelation 12. That's why we have Jesus Christ, standing at the right hand of the Father as our great Intercessor and Advocate, defending us. It's constantly going on in the heavenly realm, Satan pointing out our sin, and Jesus saying that His blood and righteousness covered that sin.

Unfortunately for Satan, he can only be in one place at one time. He's not omnipresent. And because he is limited, he has enlisted many helpers in his attack on Christ's Church. And almost all of those helpers are unsuspecting of the terrible part they play in destroying the effectiveness of other believers, of church leaders, and of the ministries of entire churches.

After thirty-plus years as a minister of God's Word, I've never seen anything as deadly to a church as the devil, the slanderer, enlisting gossiping believers to become tools in his hands. They begin to slander other believers, and they begin to tear down biblical leaders in Christ's Church, and by their accusations, they sometimes neutralize an entire local church. It's happened in every town.

We become those unwitting, unsuspecting tools, pawns in the devil's hands when we live out his name, the devil, *diabolous*. When we gossip, accuse, and slander, we act like a little devil, a little follower of the Great Accuser himself. He's been falsely accusing believers since the beginning, and every time we open our mouth to falsely accuse another believer, we are doing the devil's work.

Satan is the ultimate source of all evil, he's the root of all wrong behavior, and because, as James tells us, the tongue is capable of causing great evil, every time you and I open our mouth, the Great Accuser is close at hand, looking for a spare tongue to use for his purposes. He is at the root of all harmful talk, and all slander. And if you are damaging the reputation or ministry of others, you are a tool of the devil.

This is what Paul says should never happen in the life of a woman of grace. "The older women likewise, that they be reverent in behavior, not slanderers."[11]

Perhaps the single most powerful member of our whole body is our tongue. With it we can bless God, worship God, lead immortal souls to God through speaking and sharing His Word. We can help, we can strengthen, we can comfort. Or we can lower ourselves to be a tool of the devil. We can accuse and slander and maliciously gossip and set fires. And those fires are so destructive and so powerful because, as God's Word says, they're set on fire by hell. And every godly woman of every age determines to have this

---

11   Titus 2:3

verse, Titus 2:3, on her heart before she says another word. And she says, "Lord, I never want to be a tool with what I say in the devil's hands. I want to be full of grace, seasoned with salt, so that every time I speak, I speak as the oracle of God. Use my tongue, my lips, my voice for You alone."

The Power of the Tongue

Pastor James of the first church in Jerusalem, Jesus' earthly brother, wrote the first New Testament epistle, and in it is the premier passage on the dangers of the tongue. He explains that our words and our talking can either be the most constructive or the most destructive of all our activities.

"For we all stumble in many things. If anyone does not stumble in word, he is a perfect man, able also to bridle the whole body. Indeed, we put bits in the horses' mouths that they may obey us, and we turn their whole body. Look also at the ships: although they are so large and are driven by fierce winds, they are turned by a very small rudder wherever the pilot desires. Even so the tongue is a little member and boasts great things."[12]

Right after the wholehearted, permeating-your-behavior, every-part-of-the-life dedication to God, Paul turns the spotlight on the hardest part of the body to control. You can always tell the level of a believer's maturity by how well they control their tongue. A tongue out of control indicates a life out of control, and both cause much destruction.

A person who has learned to stop words before they come out and to think about what they say before they say it, that person, with that discipline, is also able to bridle the rest of their body. That's why, for a godly woman to be useful, she starts with the behavior of total presentation of herself to the Lord, the reverent and priest-like behavior, and the very next thing she does is to check her tongue at the door.

"See how great a forest a little fire kindles! And the tongue is a fire, a world of iniquity. The tongue is so set among our members that it defiles the whole body, and sets on fire the course of nature; and it is set on fire by hell."[13]

Note that the source of the uncontrolled tongue, James says, is hell. When someone causes fires with their mouth, when they cause problems,

---

12 James 3:2–5
13 James 3:5–6

when they stir things up, when, like in Proverbs, the talebearer keeps adding wood to the fire so it can't go out, when they go around inciting things, and say, "Did you know about this? Are you sure about that? Have you considered this?"—and it doesn't have to be a lie, just a well-placed question.

Satan can't be everywhere. He can't do everything. But he knows that if he can enlist believers to unwittingly do his work for him, he can sit back and let a church destroy itself. And if he can get control of the rudder of the ship, get ahold of that bridle in the horse's mouth, if he can ignite a believer's tongue for his purposes, he can steer the whole life of a believer away from usefulness to Christ and leave us neutralized. He can't destroy us, because we're sealed with the Holy Spirit. But he can neutralize us and even use us against other believers if he can just get ahold of that tongue.

The Tongue Set on Fire by Hell

Gossip comes in many forms, and all should be avoided by anyone seeking to be a godly Titus 2 man or woman. Gossip is a type of talk that hurts, and all of us, but especially those godly older women, should seek to avoid every type of gossip at all costs.

First, there's malicious gossip. That's what 1 Timothy 3:11 talks about. It's geared to cut, to destroy, to divide friends, to break friendships, to erode trust. That's the fire in James 3. It's someone who goes in and, in their heart, they know when they launch that flamethrower it's going to start burning, and people are going to think less of someone.

We usually think of this kind of talk as reserved for kids in high school, vying for attention and relationships, so they purposefully tear down and slander someone else. But malicious talk doesn't end in high school. It continues through life. Intentionally poisoning the waters, just to ruin people. Of course that's wrong.

But that's not the only kind of gossip. The second kind is rationalized gossip, and now we're getting into fertile ground for the Church. Often we have a little check in our spirit, and we wonder if we should say it, but we go ahead and share it anyway. Just between you and me, let's pray about this. Are you aware of what's going on?

This is still gossip that harms and that is empowered by the devil, but it comes packaged as a prayer request. This is when someone is convinced and has deceived themselves that they need to share some information for the good of another person. Often they say, "I want you to pray about something."

Do you know what encourages gossip? Accepting it. Listening to it. We're curious, so we just don't say anything. But that just adds fuel to the fire. Have you ever read Psalm 15? A godly person has a rule that they live by. They will not take up a reproach against a friend. It's hanging out there to grab, and they say, no. I can't accept that, I won't listen to that. I'm not part of the problem, I'm not part of the solution, I don't need to hear this.

If someone starts sharing with you a prayer request that you should not be hearing, just stop it in its tracks. Don't let them flame-throw all over you. Don't add wood to the fire. Send them to talk to that person, the one they're talking about, and if they've already done that, then you can go with them to talk to the person face-to-face, but don't take up a reproach against a friend.

Probably the most common kind of gossip is what I call innocent gossip. It usually starts with proper motives and desires, but gets off course. It's the unwise sharing of sensitive information. And usually the person starts feeling bad because they keep letting out stuff they shouldn't have said. And then they regret having said it, and hope it doesn't get back to the person they were talking about, but it's too late to take it back.

I used to be a youth pastor, and when you're a youth pastor, you have to come up with ways to keep their attention. So, I was in a room, with all these third through sixth graders all packed in there with me, and I had this little handful of baby powder in my hand. And I said, "You know, whenever you say something, it's like this," and then I blew into my hand, and the powder just went everywhere. And I said, "Okay, now try to collect it."

See, it was all contained before I launched it. But once it's out there, you can't ever collect all that powder. And that's just like our words. You can say you didn't mean to say that, you can say, "Let me take that back," but you can't take it back. You can't collect all those words.

It's been estimated that from our first "good morning" to our last "good night," the average person speaks the equivalent of fifty pages of a normal book. That would be two hundred books every single year if our words were all written down. And every time one of those words starts to come out, the devil is close at hand with a flamethrower ready to set on fire the things we say to tear down God's people.

The danger is even greater for godly older women. Women talk more than men, on average, but an older woman, who's already raised her children, who has spare time on her hands, has even greater potential to become what 1 Timothy 3:11 calls a "malicious talker." When Paul warns Timothy about this, he says watch out. They are idle, with too much time on their hands, and they go from house to house. They get a little here, and share a little there, and pretty soon they are speaking in a way that is malicious, that is not beneficial to the Church.

And that was in the first century. Can you imagine how much greater the temptation is today? We don't have to go from house to house. We just have to pull out our cell phone. You can be on your cell phone all day long, getting a little here, sharing little there, piecing it all together. See, the more time we have to talk, the more pages we write in our books, the more unguarded words we have that can be grasped as tools in Satan's hands.

My good friend John MacArthur says, "Whereas men tend to be rough or violent in their actions, women have a tendency to be rough or violent in their words. Older women who find themselves with time on their hands can be tempted to allow their conversations to lead to gossip and to criticism and inevitably to slander."[14]

Godly Titus 2 women are never to surrender their tongue to the devil. "Not devils," Titus 2:3. "Not little slanderers." Not little sharers and spreaders of things that shouldn't be talked about, things that are unverified, probably not true, motivations unknown, and accusations that should not be made.

Your communication either qualifies you or disqualifies you. Both times Paul zeros in on the speech of godly older women, it's in the context of what qualifies them for ministry. And he says that your ministry will be discredited if you do not have a guarded tongue. That's why Satan is so very much at work in our talk.

---

14   John MacArthur, *Different By Design* (Wheaton,: Victor Books) Marriage and Divorce (electronic edition), Logos.

Do you understand how deadly this can be? The damage that can be done? If this godly older woman is going into homes, coming right alongside these younger women to mentor and lead and go with her through life, teaching her to love her husband, to love her children, then imagine the damage if she leaves that home and goes to the next one and says, "Oh, you should see what's going on at so-and-so's house. If you only knew…"

And all of a sudden there is irreparable damage. It hurts the person she's talking about, it hurts the person spreading the gossip, and it also hurts the listener. Slander divides friends. It spreads confusion. It damages reputations and relationships, and when you share gossip with someone, you are spraying them with a flamethrower.

A Guard Over the Door of My Lips

David is called the man after God's own heart, and he models the ultimate use of the mouth, the tongue, and the words. Psalm 141:3 is God's desire for each of us, that we make this our habit. "Set a guard, O Lord, over my mouth." David is saying that his tongue is so powerful he can't guard it himself. It's so volatile, so deadly, it's like a flamethrower and it can just start fires all over the place. He needs God to do the guarding. So he says, "Keep watch over the door of my lips."

David gets even more to the point in Psalm 39:1. "I said, 'I will guard my ways, lest I sin with my tongue; I will restrain my mouth with a muzzle.'" This is what we should all be crying to God. We should be asking God for a muzzle.

How do we do that? How do we set a guard over our mouth? Do you know what a guard does? He stands at the gate or at the door and he checks credentials. You want to pass through here? You have to have the right ID. You don't get to just roll on through. You have to stop, and you're checked, and if you're qualified to pass by, then you're allowed to go on.

If you want to guard your tongue, think first. As you're opening your mouth to speak, pause a few seconds and ask, are these words true or false, accurate or exaggerated, healing or cutting, grateful or complaining? Check the credentials. Should these words be allowed to pass?

And you can't do that if you don't pause and think about it first. So, number one, to set a guard over the door of your lips, think first.

Secondly, speak less. Ecclesiastes 5:2–3 says, "Do not be rash with your mouth, and let not your heart utter anything hastily before God. For God is in heaven, and you are on earth; therefore let your words be few."

God says be quick to hear and slow to what? Speak. And be even slower to share. In fact, one of the best ways to know if you should share or not, if the person you're talking about were standing right there, would you still say it? But even more important than them standing right there is God, in heaven, listening to every one of your words.

It's a biblical fact that the less you say the wiser you appear. Proverbs 17:28 says you can even be a fool, but if you say nothing at all, they'll think you're a genius. You want to really be thought of as a wise spiritual person? Pause. Don't gush. And when in doubt, when you don't know if what you're going to say will cut or heal, if it's true or not, then it's safer not to say anything at all. In an abundance of words there is more opportunity to be a tool for the devil's use, so speak less.

But David, the man after God's own heart, who models better than anybody how to guard the tongue, also wrote some of the most widely used words in the world. They're some of the most encouraging words ever written. When people are on their deathbeds, they read Psalm 23. When they're sick, discouraged, or depressed, whose words do we read to them? David's words from the Psalms. David said a lot.

David was a man after God's own heart because he was willing to surrender his words to the Lord. He was constantly asking God to muzzle his mouth, to guard his tongue. He wanted his words used. And his words are some of the most used words in the Bible because he was very cautious with what he said.

Do you know what happens when we have a guarded, muzzled, and surrendered tongue? We become useful to God instead of the devil. See, we're all useful. It can either be to God, or to the devil. There's no middle ground.

Do you remember Samuel? I love what God's Word says about Samuel. Not one of his words fell to the ground. Every single word he said landed, hit its target, and was useful to God. When I memorized that verse, it was fall, and the leaves were a foot thick on the ground, and I imagined how many of my words just fall to the ground useless, lying there like leaves ready to be raked up and burned. But Samuel's words, every one of them, was useful to God. They didn't fall to the ground.

Do you want to be someone whose words are useful to God? Pray, prepare, plan, concentrate. Enrich every opportunity you have to speak. Make every time you speak a 1 Peter 4:11 moment. Listen to how Peter, the apostle with the foot-shaped mouth, grew in his understanding of godly talk. If you're going to speak, 1 Peter 4:11, "let it be as an oracle of God."

Do you know what an oracle is? It's someone who speaks on behalf of God. They'd stand in the town square, blow the trumpet, everyone would get quiet, and they'd stand there until they had the absolute attention of everyone, and they would speak on behalf of their god.

It keeps going back to this concept, of being a representative of God. The godly older woman is to be reverent in all her behavior, first of all, but now, even with the words she speaks, it's like God is the One speaking. You flip open your phone, you hit that speed dial, you hear a familiar voice at the other end, just before you launch into whatever you were going to say, in your heart, say, "I'm speaking as an oracle of God." That might just curtail what you were going to say.

Peter says that every time we speak, we are to speak as God's mouthpiece. That should be the primary motivation for everything we say, because they're the words God wants said. Think for a second. Would God's oracle say that? Would God's oracle share that? Would God's oracle present this? Communicate this? If the trumpet is blown and everyone is listening for the words to come from God, would these words be what He wants said?

How do you know what words God wants said? Well, when in doubt, don't say anything at all because God hears and you can't take it back, but God has actually told us what His words sound like.

See, there are only two sources to download your words from. The motivation for what we say can come either from below, that's Satan's realm, or from above, that's God's realm. They either come as words from God, or from Satan. And our words are either useful to God, or to Satan. And we can tell where our words are emanating from by the results.

Think about the results your words have. "This wisdom does not descend from above, but is earthly, sensual, demonic." How can you tell? "For where envy and self-seeking exist, confusion and every evil thing are there." Do you know what prompts a lot of bad talk, slander, and gossip? Jealousy. Envy. Self-seeking. Is your talk motivated by jealousy or envy? Are you seeking to serve self? Does your speech cause confusion? Division? Then it's not from God. Whenever what we say causes this list of woes from James 3:15–16, whenever what we say causes jealousy or envy or evil practice, God hasn't prompted our words. We are not walking in the Spirit. We are not energized by His grace.

"But the wisdom that is from above is first pure, then peaceable, gentle, willing to yield, full of mercy and good fruits, without partiality and without hypocrisy." And you know what "good fruits" are? "Now the fruit of righteousness is sown in peace by those who make peace."[15] You'll know the source of your words, what prompts them, by the results. Do your words result in peace?

Are your words pure? Do they lead to peaceable responses? Do your words hammer people or are they gentle? Do your words show a willingness to yield? Are they full of mercy? Do they produce the fruit of righteousness and peace? Are they unbiased, without partiality? Without hypocrisy? If the words are mixed with an improper motivation, stop them at the gate. Don't let them through. If they're hypocritical, refuse to let them pass.

Set a guard over the door of your lips. Only allow to spring forth from your lips what is pleasing to God, the words He would speak, downloaded from above, not from Satan's realm. And make sure that every word that tries to pass through that door of your lips meets the qualifications for an oracle of God.

> Lord, my words can be used for You. You collect my words, all my prayers, my worship in Your bowl. Lord, I want to be renewed. Guard my mouth, muzzle me. When I speak corruptly, harshly, maliciously, Lord, I want to put that off. Strip off the old way I was, Lord. Renew my mind. I want to speak the way You speak, that

---

15   James 3:17–18

when You spoke on this earth, people said no one ever spoke like You because Your words were so gracious. Lord, put that on me. As Your representative, I want to surrender to You daily. I can't decide today that I will never say another wrong thing for the rest of my life, but I can, today, decide to surrender my tongue to You for right now. Let me speak as Your oracle so that not a single word falls to the ground. In Your precious name, I pray, amen.

Respond to Truth

What things come out of a mouth surrendered to God (Joshua 1:8; Psalm 32:3–5; Psalm 77:12; Luke 1:64; Romans 10:9–10; Ephesians 4:29; 1 Peter 3:9)?

What things come out of a mouth surrendered to the devil (Psalm 10:7; Psalm 109:3; Proverbs 6:12; Proverbs 12:22; Proverbs 15:2; Proverbs 15:28; Proverbs 26:28; Romans 1:28–30; Ephesians 4:29)?

Today, what kind of words did you speak? (Matthew 12:34; Luke 6:45; Philippians 4:8)

If the words you speak don't edify, uplift, or in some other way point people to God, if they're not spoken as God's oracle, what happens (Matthew 12:36)?

When in your life or in your schedule have you realized you were most vulnerable to being used as a tool in the devil's hands? How can you specifically guard your mouth in those moments?

What two things should characterize our speech (Ephesians 4:15)? What does love do (1 Corinthians 13:6)? What does truth do (1 Peter 1:22)?

Women Who Are Addicted to God | 4

The world of the New Testament, including the group of new believers Paul was writing to on Crete, was dominated by the Roman Empire. It was an era in history when most people lived short and unusually hard lives of physical labor, emotional stress, and poor health. They were in an empire, highly taxed, highly regulated, and struggling through life. Most people worked very hard and didn't live past their fifties.

Paul's third admonition to godly women directly addresses the world they lived in. Much like some cultures today, where life is hard, drinking was the norm in the Roman Empire. And especially for women, drinking wine was very often the only escape they had from their hard lives. But this third admonition is not limited to first-century Crete. This is for every-century people of God. Why? Because this admonition, more than any other, determines our eternal rewards. In fact, 1 Corinthians 9:24–27 promises a crown given to those who spend their lives denying the flesh, disciplining their appetites in order to be enslaved to God only. And that's what Titus 2:3 is about.

"The older women, likewise, that they be reverent in behavior, not slanderers, not given to much wine."

These godly women were formerly pagans, living in a culture where drinking was accepted, expected, and simply a way of life. It was the best way to forget about their problems of being enslaved to a pagan man who looked on his wife only as a convenience who bore him legitimate children and enhanced his standing in the community. That's all a woman was back then. She wasn't even supposed to leave the house. She was just supposed to be there for whatever he wanted.

Hopelessness for these women led to drunkenness. That's why Paul says to the Ephesians that before they knew Christ, they were "without Christ, having no hope and without God in the world."[16] These women were formerly hopeless and godless, so of course they turned to wine to dull their pain, and God's grace changed all that. But even after the grace of God gloriously saved them, old habits were hard to break. The old ways of their husbands would come back. The old pains of emotional and physical abuse would resurface. The temptation to slip back into the intemperance of slavery to wine would grow strong.

In all the dark struggles of first century life, there was one bright spot for most people, and that bright spot was the warming glow of drinking wine. After a few swallows, their troubles would seem to drift away. Their cares would begin to evaporate. Their aches and pains lessened until they almost vanished. They were still living in that hard world, but all of it seemed to get better. Briefly.

But as all their problems were drifting away, their minds would get clouded, their discipline was abandoned, and their behavior became unrestrained. The downside of alcohol is the deadly effect of loosening inhibitions, of discipline being abandoned, and the lurking power of getting addicted to the warming glow it brings. Then of course there's the inevitable surrender to the desires of the flesh.

I remember when I was a salesman in the eighties, I was flying back and forth between the world's most conservative seminary, and the world's least conservative sales environment in Los Angeles, California. I was just a short-term salesman and could earn 60 percent of my annual salary in a bonus that they'd give at these elaborate parties. So I flew to the party, but I'd never been to one of those before. Thousands of people in a mega banquet hall, and the lights went down, the music started pulsating, and everyone started drinking. And pretty soon they were standing on the tables and

---

16 Ephesians 2:12

dancing. These cultured, refined, white-shirted businessmen were dancing on the tables, falling down, spilling their drinks, with their arms around people they were not married to.

That's why Proverbs warns repeatedly against drunkenness, and the dangers and corrosiveness of alcohol. God has always affirmed that wine is a mocker, that the pleasures of sin are fleeting, and that giving ourselves over to drinking, or any kind of ungodly activity that's addictive, can satisfy our souls briefly, but it's like being adrift in the ocean, dying of thirst, and drinking salt water to quench that thirst. The more you drink salt water, the thirstier you are, the stronger the burn gets. The more alcohol you drink, the more you need it. The more drugs you use, the more you want it. And the more addictive behaviors you have, the more you do them.

Now, for us, "not given to much wine," seems like a strange thing to put on the list of qualities for a godly woman. After all, when was the last time you heard of a reverent, godly older woman who was given to much wine? It's probably not a problem that's on the forefront of most of our minds, but Paul zeroes in on the self-disciplined life of moderation that is to characterize every woman of every age in Christ's Church.

Today, "not given to much wine" goes so far beyond just drinking wine. Today there are so many forms of alcohol never even imagined in biblical times. The highest strength alcohol they had would be modern-day brandy. They knew nothing of distilled spirits or all the incredible levels of alcohol that have been cultivated in modern times.

Wine was the easiest and most convenient thing you could be addicted to back then, but Paul is warning about so much more than just wine. Drugs, both legal and illegal, can be abused. Tobacco can be abused. Wonderful varieties of food can be abused. There are beautiful varieties of fashionable clothing that you can change every season, and people can be enslaved to that. We can be enslaved to our house, to every recreational thing. Anything can become an addiction. "Not given to much wine" means, literally, "not enslaved," and this "not given to much wine" is a refusal to be enslaved by anything.

There's a whole generation of believers who have never tasted a drop of alcohol and pride themselves on that choice while overeating with daily regularity. Did you know that, side-by-side in Proverbs, when God condemns alcohol consumption and drunkenness, He condemns overeating in the same breath? We condemn the abuse of alcohol and yet are totally enslaved to other appetites.

Modern society has elevated fashion to almost the point of idolatry. Clothing stores and newspapers and magazine advertisements and television commercials are like giant billboards that continually proclaim "We covet clothing." And if you don't have this clothing or look like that, you're nothing. Expensive, often ostentatious jewelry is becoming more prevalent as more and more flaunt their material prosperity and glorify themselves. We are constantly goaded to put our bodies and apparel on parade.

Godly older women don't do that.

We must be as cautious about any intemperance, not be given to too much of anything, be it the use of money, the enjoyment of leisure, the establishment of a house to live in, nothing. Whatever we do is to be tempered by the glory of God. He must be the object and focus of everything we do. Do you remember what Paul concluded his discussion of Christian liberty with? "Therefore, whether you eat or drink, or whatever you do, do all to the glory of God."[17]

Remember what Paul said to the Ephesians? "And do not be drunk with wine, in which is dissipation; but be filled with the Spirit."[18] You can't be controlled by wine and by the Spirit at the same time. You can't serve two masters. Either you're enslaved to your appetites, whether for alcohol or drugs or status or pleasure or comfort and convenience, or you're a slave to the Holy Spirit.

Godly women are Spirit-led in every area of their lives. They are not slaves to any substance, any amusement, any fashion, or any attitude that does not please their master in heaven. Lack of physical control of any appetite points to spiritual immaturity, so mature, godly women say, "I will not allow anything on the outside to control me on the inside."

I had a friend who would try to go without things, just to see if he could. He'd go a week without television, just to be sure that he could say

---

17   1 Corinthians 10:31
18   Ephesians 5:18

no to that. Then he'd go a week without sports, and then a week without whatever. He didn't want to be controlled by anything but God. Everything in life, he could give up, except for God. And that's the choice a woman of grace makes, that nothing in life will control her except God.

Discipline is saying no to something you could say yes to. Many people say no to things for their health, for their liver, or for the glow of their skin. But when you say no to something for God, that gets eternal rewards. The Bible never forbids wine drinking in moderation, but we see from Romans 14 and 1 Corinthians 8 that our liberty is limited by the consciences of other believers and our testimony to the world. And so with this warning, God is presenting the godly women of Titus 2 with a choice that will shape their lives, and that choice will determine, not just the course of their lives here on earth, but their eternal rewards in heaven.

A Lifestyle of Personal Discipline

The godly woman of Titus 2 is a Spirit-controlled woman in every part of her life. In an undisciplined world, surrounded by people dancing on the tables, she lives a lifestyle of personal discipline, and because of that, God offers to her a crown. And He's offering the same crown today to anyone who will deny their flesh.

The Apostle Paul makes a shocking self-disclosure in 1 Corinthians 9. This is the Apostle Paul who was personally discipled by Jesus Christ. Jesus went soul-winning and knocked him off his horse to get his attention, and he was personally taught for three years in the back side of the desert by Jesus Christ Himself. He got his own tour of heaven and couldn't even tell us what he saw. What he wrote and what was written about him makes up a third of the New Testament. He was the quintessential, hand-picked servant of God. This man was stellar.

But he's urging the Corinthians to discipline themselves for godliness, and he says, "Do you not know that those who run in a race all run, but one receives the prize? Run in such a way that you may obtain it. And everyone who competes for the prize is temperate in all things. Now they do it to obtain a perishable crown, but we for an imperishable crown. Therefore, I run thus: not with uncertainty. Thus I fight; not as one who beats the air," and here's what's shocking: "But I discipline my body and bring it into subjection, lest, when I have preached to others, I myself should be disqualified."[19]

Paul? Disqualified? Really? Even though he was personally taught by Jesus, wrote Scripture, and saw heaven, he knew that he couldn't just sit back on his past accomplishments and coast to the finish line. So what does he do? He runs to win the "prize," verse 25.

The word is *agonizumi.* That's how the Greek games were described in the first century. Agonizing. You had to run with agony to win the prize. That's what my cross-country coach used to call "eating your guts," running until you vomited. You had to be ruthlessly in control of yourself. So for Paul to get the prize, the *agonizumi,* he had to be temperate in all things. That's where the crown comes from.

In the Greek games, do you know what they got? They got a little laurel branch, and the judges would clip them off the tree, twist them into a crown shape, and that little circle of leaves was all you got for eating your guts. It was perishable. After a few days, the leaves would shrivel and dry up, the bugs would get in it, and it would die.

But we agonize for an imperishable crown. Therefore, Paul runs a certain way. He fights a certain way. He disciplines his body because he wants to get that crown.

The word "discipline" is a fascinating word. *Hupopiadzo.* To hit under the eye. I'm not a boxer, but my father was a boxer in this coal-mining town, and my older brother and father both were golden gloves guys. I was more the golden pencil guy, so I only fought once, and I did what my dad said and it was so horrible, when I hit that guy like my dad taught me, I saw the blood and I never did it again. But that's the picture Paul is painting of this brutal self-discipline. He doesn't hit other people. He disciplines himself.

So Paul is saying that he punches himself underneath the eye, beating his body into submission. Again, he's referencing the Pan-Isthmian games. First a race, now boxing. And he brutally brings his body into subjection, *doulogogo,* to make his body a slave. He's making the choice that he will not be ruled by his body, by his appetites. He will show his body who is in control.

---

19   1 Corinthians 9:24-27

The Christian life is described by God, in other parts of the New Testament, as an agonizing race, as a grueling wrestling match. But here in these verses, spiritual living is compared to a painful boxing ring. And we have to give our own flesh knockout blows so we don't get thrown out of the ring. In these games, it didn't matter if you won first place. If you hit below the belt, you were disqualified. If you drifted out of your lane, you were out, just like that. You could be the fastest, the strongest, the best runner in the whole thing, but if you broke a rule, crossed over the line, you were disqualified.

Paul realized that he had a traitor here. His flesh. And our flesh longs for everything the world, the flesh, and the devil has to offer. It all looks so attractive, and the world is saying, come on, just have some of this, it's no big deal, you only go around once. And Paul is saying you're going to waste your life. It won't last. And you'll be disqualified.

Paul, who knew the Lord, suffered for decades, and loved God with all his heart said that if he did not stay vigilant, his traitorous flesh in a moment of weakness would betray him, and he might get out of his lane in the race for the Lord and get ejected. That's sobering.

Our life is summed up in 1 Corinthians 9:24–27 as a lifelong struggle not to be enslaved by our appetites, but to be surrendered to God. Women of grace are restrained by the grace of God from choosing to feed their appetites with anything that doesn't please Him. They don't even go near those things. For the Titus 2 woman of grace, there is no appetite in life greater than her appetite for God.

Pop Quiz for Loving God Most

Can you honestly say that your appetite for pleasing God is stronger than your desire for anything else? If we could see your heart and mind and habits as God sees them, all those daily choices that God is weighing and either rewarding or discarding, what would we find? Only things that reflect your addiction to the Lord? Would we find that there are no idols you're secretly hiding and secretly sacrificing your time and money for instead of for God?

Do you know what an idol was? It was something people thought would give them benefits, so they sacrificed God for that. It doesn't have to be carved, and it doesn't have to be on your shelf. It's when we sacrifice what belongs to God for something else. That, whatever it is, becomes an idol. It's a humanly made object or practice that we turn to instead of God.

Typical American idols are the media, we listen to music more than we listen to God; money, we trust in our wealth and jobs more than we trust in God, who gives us life and strength; our appearance, we're more concerned about our clothes and our looks than our spiritual condition; status, we sacrifice to have things and pleasures and experiences that don't please God; or our personal agenda, we sacrifice the eternal time with God, His Word, His Church, and His ministry for the temporal. Our schedules are filled with sports and amusements and pleasures and even sinful activities, all of which crowd out God.

We are to seek God ahead of every other option. That's why He says, "seek first the kingdom of God and His righteousness."[20] Seek second? Third? When you find the time? No. He says seek first. God told the church in Ephesus they had left their first love. It didn't mean they didn't love Him. They loved everything. They'd just stopped loving Him first.

We still live everyday life. We still go to work. We still wash the dishes. But there is a higher calling, and that calling is to seek first God's lordship, God's rule, over everything else.

I remember back in school, I had this teacher who would start every class with, "Okay, take out a half a sheet of paper," and we'd have a pop quiz. Unannounced, on the spot, three questions, put your name at the top. Well, let's do a pop quiz from God, for every woman who wants to get an eternal reward from God.

1. **Possessions.** Are you more excited about going shopping and acquiring more beautiful things than you are about transforming more things on earth into things that will be your offering of worship to God in heaven?

Jesus very clearly tells us shopping is okay as long as the things we're shopping for are for heaven. Not stacking things here on earth. "Do not lay up for yourselves treasures on earth." Why? Because the moths will eat it,

---

20 Matthew 6:33

the rust will ruin it, and the thieves will break in and steal it. "But," and this is a command, "lay up for yourselves treasures in heaven, where neither moth nor rust destroy and where thieves do not break in and steal." Well, that's nice, but why is that important? "For where your treasure is, there your heart will be also."[21]

I used to work as a butler for a very wealthy neurosurgeon and his wife, and at one point, their house was basically a little Louvre. He was making $7,000 an hour and had to use it, so they had nine fireplaces, and over every one was this masterpiece all lit up. They had original paintings from all over the world.

So one time they took me out to dinner and we were just getting our meal, and we'd prayed, and we were about to cut into those perfect steaks when the Mrs. said to the Mr., "You set the alarm, didn't you?" And he said, "No. You set the alarm."

I'll always remember the sound of silverware dropping and the chairs shoving back from the table as they both ran to the car to get home and set the alarm. Why? Because thieves break in and steal.

Isn't it sad to spend your life for something that someone will just steal one day, or the government will get away from you by taxation, or that death will wrestle out of your hands? When we have the opportunity to lay up for ourselves treasures in heaven?

But possessions aren't the only thing that wrestle first place away from God.

2. **Sacrifices.** Are you more committed to school, work, and sports events than you are to God, His Word, and Christ as His Church gathers? Is your life running at full speed and it seems that your family life, your devotional life, and your ministry life are all waning but your activities are actually increasing?

Women of grace do not sacrifice the eternal on the altar of the temporary. In Romans 12:1, Paul defines where we are to sacrifice, and it's for Christ and His eternal priorities, not earth and temporary ones.

---

21 Matthew 6:19–21

Did you know we're supposed to do a reset every so often? Just stop everything and evaluate? We have friends who, several years ago, had a motorhome they'd let us use because our eight kids wouldn't all fit in the car, and it was really neat. It had a shower and a washer and dryer and it slid out in all directions, and it was really fun. But when that thing was going seventy miles an hour on the turnpike, if you ever stepped on the brake, everything that wasn't nailed down would go flying into the windshield at seventy miles an hour.

Sometimes we need to put the brakes on in life and stop, and look to see if all the stuff that's hurtling through at rapid speeds even pleases God. Sometimes we're going along so fast we haven't even checked to see if all the things we're sacrificing for are even nailed down, if they'll last when God throws the brakes on.

And this is the reset button, the brakes, the test: "I beseech you therefore, brethren, by the mercies of God, that you present your bodies a living sacrifice, holy, acceptable to God."[22]

We sacrifice for a lot of things, our jobs, our sports and schools and schedules and everything else. Do you know who you're really supposed to be sacrificing for? God. Make sure what you're sacrificing for is holy and acceptable to God.

3. **Beauty.** Are you more faithful to the exercise, beautification, and care of your physical body than you are to the nurture of your spiritual soul?

Women of grace are not addicted to their temporal beauty. First Peter 3:3–4 is where Peter explains that real beauty is spiritual, and it's to take priority over passing, momentary, earthly beauty. "Do not let your adornment be *merely...*" In other words, adorn. There's nothing wrong with adornment, but don't let it be merely on the outside. Don't focus your life on external beauty.

"Do not let your adornment be merely outward—arranging the hair, wearing gold, or putting on fine apparel—rather let it be the hidden

---

22 Romans 12:1

person of the heart, with the incorruptible beauty of a gentle and quiet spirit, which is very precious in the sight of God."

Let the spiritual person, that you nurture from the Word of God and prayer and worship, be what you adorn. And you will gain the incorruptible beauty of a gentle and quiet spirit, which is precious to God.

If you spend the majority of your time and earthly attention making sure you're as gorgeous as possible externally, and because there's such a focus on externals that you neglect the spiritual, then you are not disciplining your appetites. You're allowing your appetite for the external preempt and supersede your appetite for God.

4. **Communication.** Are you more connected with your friends on social media, your pictures and your scrapbooks, than you are connected with the One who bought you with His own blood? Do you share more about yourself and your every movement, every thought, and every picture with others than you share with your God whose greatness surpasses life?

I believe there are women who are addicted to social media instead of to loving their Master in heaven, their husbands, and their children. Someday in the hospital, as you breathe your last breath, you will not be wishing you had posted one more update. You will be wishing you'd spent more time loving God, serving Him, and loving your family.

Women of grace are not addicted to their temporal communications. "Behold, I stand at the door and knock. If anyone hears My voice and opens the door, I will come in to him and dine with him, and he with Me."

In Revelation 3:20, Jesus is standing outside the busy life of believers saying, "Hey, got any time to spend with Me? Behold, I stand at the door of your busy life, and I'm knocking. I want to come in and dine with you." That's about devotions. That's about communication with God.

Jesus is knocking. Wanting you to turn that off, to get up for a second, to open the door and pay attention to Him. People have time for everything they really want to do. What do you want? Eternal rewards? Or temporary pleasures? To go shopping for moth-eaten, rusted, insecure possessions, or to start shipping your possessions ahead to heaven? To make sacrifices for the temporal? Or for the eternal? To have a beautiful earthly body that will fade and wrinkle with age, or an imperishable beauty that only grows more precious as time goes by? Connection with the thousand friends you barely know or don't even know at all? Or a connection with the One who died for you, who's knocking, whose grace brings salvation, and teaches us to deny ourselves and our lusts in order to earn eternal rewards?

When I was eleven years old, I used to work at a tomato farm in Lansing, Michigan, and there was this elderly woman who owned the tomato farm. My parents would drop me off, and I carried around this can of gasoline, and my job was to pick off the spiky green tomato worms and drop them into the gasoline, and that would kill them instantly. And this lady would follow me with her yardstick, and when I wasn't picking fast enough, she'd whack me with the yardstick. "I'm paying you thirty-five cents an hour," *whack*, "pick more worms."

Grace is not like that. Grace doesn't go around with a yardstick saying, "Spend less time with makeup." *Whack*. "Spend more time in prayer." But these are things for us to think about. It's not that we can't have possessions or make sacrifices. It's that we love God and want to please Him because what pleases Him will last forever, so that's what we want to spend our time doing.

Grace teaches us to *arneomai*, deny, or "refuse, reject, not accept, not take the offer of" any form of ungodliness the world has to offer. It's the same word used for Peter when he "denied" Christ. He wanted nothing to do with Christ, refused even to be associated with Him. The same word is used for Moses, who refused to be called the son of Pharaoh's daughter. He cut off all contact. That's what grace, like a loving parent training a child, teaches us to do.

God puts this quality in the middle of His five desires for godly older women, I believe, because it affects, more than any other, whether you get an unfading crown to throw at Jesus' feet. An undisciplined life affects the reverent behavior, it affects the quality of our words, it affects the exemplary life we're supposed to live, and it affects the teaching older women are supposed to do. If you don't get this one under control, you'll have nothing. But if you have disciplined yourself and brought your appetites under control, then you will have unfading crowns to throw at Jesus' feet.

> *Father in heaven, I thank You that You speak and Your Word is clear. And I pray that we will respond. We don't want to be addicted to anything. There are so many more things than just these mentioned, that Your Spirit can convict us about, that we can respond to. We want to seek You first, seek You with all our heart, and never leave You outside knocking. You can dine with me anytime. Thank You for Your love, Your patience, for being the God of new beginnings. Change many minds today for your glory. In Jesus' name I pray, amen.*

Respond to Truth

Make a list of your daily activities starting with what takes up the most time at the top, and what you give least time to at the bottom. Where does spending time with God fall on the list? Does this list show an addiction and insatiable craving for God?

What in your life can you not go a single day without? A single week? Is spending time in God's Word, in prayer, or with other believers on that list?

Where are the things you value? In your house, your garage, your closet, or in heaven waiting for you? What practical steps can you take to have your heart set on heaven (Matthew 6:19–21)?

Do you spend more time looking in the mirror over your bathroom sink, or in the mirror of God's Word each morning before you leave the house? Which concerns you more, your appearance on the outside, or your appearance on the inside? How can you devote more time to the person God sees (James 1:22–25)?

How much time do you devote to social media? What's the length of your average phone conversation? How regularly are your prayer times with God that long and uninterrupted? What can you do today to stay connected with God knowing He's the most important personal contact you have?

Modeling Godliness in a Godless World | 5

THE SIN-WARPED ISLE OF CRETE

A couple of years ago, I was invited to come and lecture a group of ninety pastors on the island of Crete. They paid my way and flew me over there, and I took all those pastors all over the island of Crete. And even though I'd never been to Crete, I had the material right in front of me, the epistle that God wrote to Crete. I'll never forget the first lecture on Crete. I was standing in the middle of this Minoan civilization, and right behind me was the alleyway that led to where the human sacrifices were done.

And I remember standing there, in front of these ninety pastors, and the first thing I said was, "When Paul wrote a letter to a pastor named Titus, who was serving on Crete…" all those ninety pastors started clucking and whispering, and finally one of them raised his hand, and asked how I know that, so I held up my Bible.

See, I didn't realize this, but in the denomination of the pastors I was teaching, they don't really use the Bible, because it can't mean what it says. It had to mean something else. And you have to work all week long and read the newspaper and read poetry and find something to say, because the Bible couldn't possibly mean what it says.

So for the rest of the week, they kept hounding me. "Do you mean that Paul wrote the book of Philippians to the church at Philippi we're going to?" "How do you know that?" And I kept going back to the Bible. Because I believe the Bible is inspired by God, breathed out, and that it does mean what it says, and that, specifically, it meant something to the real people to whom it was written to two thousand years ago. Titus 2 is not a list of guidelines Paul just dreamed up one day. He was writing God's strategy for changing real people and reaching a real place that was steeped in paganism.

Fifteen hundred years before Paul wrote to Crete, many scholars believe, people from Crete set sail and conquered and lived in Palestine, and they became known as the Philistines. These are descended from the same people. So if you want to know what Titus's congregation was like, think of Goliath, the horrible, anti-God, warring-against-God's-people culture. And it was no different in the days of Paul.

Six hundred years before Paul wrote to Crete, a pagan prophet named Epimenides said, "Cretans are always liars, evil beasts, lazy gluttons." And Paul, writing to Titus, repeats that quote, and look what Paul says: "This testimony is true."[23] How would you like to go to a group of people and say, "you are a bunch of constant liars, evil beasts and lazy gluttons"? That's the congregation, the culture that they had come to Christ from.

What a miracle to find a group of believers saved out of such a godless society. They came from a culture dominated by liars, and when Paul says "always," he's not exaggerating. In fact, the verb form of the Greek word for "Crete" means, "to lie." These were people who were also completely out of control. An evil beast is just a menace, doing whatever it wants whenever it wants to, totally out of control. And they're gluttons, characterized by the total undisciplined pursuit of their lust-filled appetites. They never have enough, and always want more and more and more.

God was calling His people to live an extraordinary spiritual life in the midst of a very unspiritual culture. They weren't supposed to move out onto another island in the middle of the Mediterranean where things weren't so bad and start a Christian commune. They had to live in that ungodly culture, so when Paul wrote about what godly older women are supposed to do, and godly older men, and younger women, and younger men, he was writing God's actual words to real people who were living in a place so

---

23 Titus 1:12–13

antagonistic to the gospel that the grace of God had to overcome every level of the culture.

When the gospel of Jesus Christ entered the Roman world of the first century, the landscape was very bleak. Christ's Church was born into a sin-warped, sin-darkened world of mixed-up marriages, sin-scarred lives, and confused families.

Men and women who were gloriously saved did not automatically become great wives and mothers, husbands and fathers. And while God gave them, at the moment of salvation, the grace they needed to live as men and women of grace, they needed to be taught, to be shown, and to have modeled for them what God's plan was for the family and the home. Men didn't know their gender-specific role as men in the home and the church. Women didn't understand their roles in the home and the church. Husbands had never heard about servant leadership. Women had never seen or even heard about the gracious Spirit-energized submission that was to be modeled for them by their mothers or other godly older women.

In the ancient paganism of the Roman world, the family was very much under attack, even more than it is today. That paganism had all but erased the plans that God had left for marriage and the family. And so, when the Church of Jesus Christ was deployed into that world, and began sharing His grace, they were charged with cultivating Christian marriages and establishing Christian homes in a culture that, at every level, was antagonistic to the cross of Christ.

The Old Testament Jewish culture had moved away from God's plan for marriage and the home. They had expanded the divorce provisions of Deuteronomy 24 to include anything a husband didn't like. By Christ's day, divorce was commonplace and expected, and a man could get a legitimate, temple-approved divorce for anything from his wife burning the toast to not looking pretty enough. Many men felt that women were only an object to be used, and a common prayer of the day that really reflected the culture's perception of women was this: God, I thank You that I'm not a Gentile, a slave, or a woman.

The secular Greek culture had further decimated the place of women. In Greek society, men were allowed to have concubines and consorts. A concubine was a regular sexual friend, and a consort was an occasional sexual friend, but all men were to maintain a wife for legitimate children. That was the culture. You had a legitimate wife for legitimate heirs for legal purposes, but that's it. So culturally, across the Greek world, women were considered little more than servants.

And in the first century Roman Empire, built on the Greek society, the family was plunged even deeper into darkness. Divorce became widespread, and as affluence increased, family life decreased. The great materialistic Roman culture with all its wealth and all its conquests elevated decadence and devalued the family to the point that many women of the Roman world chose not to even have children because it would ruin their freedom and destroy the look of their bodies.

So how did Paul deal with that? How would you reach a culture that had God's word and turned from it, a culture that said the family was nothing, a society that promoted the very dissolution of family and marriage with serial divorce?

Titus 2:11–12 says, "For the grace of God that brings salvation has appeared to all men, teaching us that, denying ungodliness and worldly lusts, we should live soberly, righteously, and godly in the present age."

Saved by His Grace, Sanctified by His Word

The word Paul uses in Titus 2:12, "teaching," is the word *piduo,* speaks of training up a child, using discipline as needed. It's actually the word for "child-ing," for teaching someone who needs to learn from the ground up. So the grace of God, verse 12, starts us out as children, and as God's grace takes us from being children into growing maturity, we learn something.

The second word that stands out in verse 12 is "denying." *Arneomai.* It means to refuse, to reject, to not accept, to not take the offer of. It means whenever sin comes knocking at the door, you do what Martin Luther used to. He would say that when sin knocks on his heart, he'd send Jesus to answer the door, and Jesus would say, "Martin doesn't live here anymore. I do."

With that same emphatic sense, God's grace teaches us, like a child, how to say no to sin. You know you're growing spiritually if you're saying no more and more to sin and yes more and more to God.

This was God's plan for penetrating the culture, His plan for seeing people go out and deny their whole way of life, their whole upbringing, the way they were raised, and to go His way. How would God get His gospel to the furthest corner of the Roman world? The plan was simple. It starts with the grace of God that brings salvation. And that same grace, the grace we do not deserve, we could not earn, and that is given as a free gift, not by trying hard, but by trusting in Jesus Christ, that grace is now deployed into our lives, to energize us, to work in us, to begin to change us from the inside out.

That's the marvel of the gospel of Jesus Christ. It's not about getting enough external influences on a person to prop them up and change them. It's not getting them to enough classes or getting them enough support. It's an internal life transformation, when God gives us a new heart. And His grace, poured out, changed people from the inside out.

The grace of God teaches us to deny ungodliness, and it empowered believers to overcome every level of the culture, but the people of Crete, living in a culture opposed to the things of God, needed to be taught, systematically, what pleases God, and what doesn't. So Paul tells Titus in Titus 2:1, to "speak the things which are proper for sound doctrine." And he ends the passage with the same command, "Speak these things, exhort, and rebuke with all authority."[24]

So it was Titus' job as pastor to teach the things which make for sound doctrine, to teach the people what God says is right and what He says is good and what He says lasts forever. His grace would be taught, modeled, and exhibited by Paul and Titus, and that would produce matured believers, but it didn't stop there. It moved down from there into the very lives of individuals in the church. Through the grace of God and the teaching of His Word, they had all they needed for life and godliness in their heads, but for them to take those principles from God's Word and put them into practice, they needed something else.

As we come to the fourth and fifth elements of a godly older woman's life, we see that Paul did not instruct Titus to teach each and every woman in the church how to, verses 4–5, "love their husbands, to love their children, to be discreet, chaste, homemakers, good, obedient to their own husbands." Instead, he was to mobilize a secondary ministry of godly older women who would seek out the younger women and show them in practical, hands-on ways, how to put into practice the things that Pastor Titus had taught.

Steeped in a family-unfriendly culture, men and women who received the grace of God at salvation did not sit under the teaching of Paul or Titus, say, "Yes, I want that," and then walk out this perfect model of a godly husband or wife, father or mother. It didn't happen that way. And it doesn't happen that way today. It's an internal change by the grace of God, and from that point on, grace begins to teach us to deny ungodliness. And as they gathered together in the corporate worship services and were taught what ungodliness God wanted them to deny, they needed that last level of training, that last level of grace-energized exemplary living that showed them how to put into practice what grace was teaching them to do.

Living for What is Good

Modeling seems to be one of the great dreams for many people in our culture today, but the best and most rewarding modeling career is with God. It's one thing to see the dress on the hanger, but when you see it on someone, then you understand how it can look on you, and you want that. And there are only two choices for what we can put on and model with our lives.

Have you ever noticed Jesus always deals in sharp contrasts and absolutes? With Jesus, there's no middle ground. That's why people didn't like Him. With a lot of people, we like to have this comfortable middle ground. We know what God says here, and we know what God says over here, but we don't really know what to do, and so we get this wide undetermined area with all this wiggle room. Jesus wasn't like that.

This is what I mean. Matthew 6:19. "Do not lay up for yourselves treasures on earth, where moth and rust destroy and where thieves break in and steal." Don't lay it up here, Jesus says. It's fine to have possessions, but the ones you treasure, the ones that you want to keep, don't lay them here, because they're going to get ruined. Put them instead in heaven, where there is no rust or moths or thieves. And the reason for this is in verse 21.

"For where your treasure is, there your heart will be also." Wherever you're laying stuff up is where your attention is going to be, and there are only two banks, where everything gets taken away from you, and where things are secure forever.

A second absolute statement, Matthew 6:24: "No one can serve two masters; for either he will hate the one and love the other, or he will be loyal to the one and despise the other." You can't serve God and anything else. There can be two masters, but only one can be loved, only one can be served, only one can be pleased by our lives. So all of life is deciding what bank you're going to use, what master you're going to serve. But He doesn't stop there.

In Matthew 7:13–14, Jesus says this: "Enter by the narrow gate; for wide is the gate and broad is the way that leads to destruction, and there are many who go in by it. Because narrow is the gate and difficult is the way which leads to life, and there are few who find it." You notice how absolute He is? You notice how everything is a strong, sharp contrast? Two choices. Clearly. Only two roads, one to heaven, one to hell. No middle road. No other way. No other choice. Heaven or hell, the bank of heaven, or the bank on earth, either God as master or anything else as master. But you can't have both.

Dawn in the northern Ontario region called Chapleau is cold! How vividly I remember that morning over 50 years ago. Pulled out of a warm sleeping bag, plunked into a cold steel canoe and now shivering in the 4 AM morning somewhere out in a vast Northern Canadian lake. There as my dad angled for muskies and walleyes, I saw something that will forever remind me of the most compelling moment every Christian will face.

Think about that. Every day, every moment, every thought, every action, every motive, is lived in front of Christ. "Therefore we make it our aim, whether present or absent, to be well pleasing to Him." Why? "For we must all appear before the judgment seat of Christ, that each one may receive the things done in the body, according to what he has done," and here are the categories: "whether good or good for nothing."

As dawn broke and the huge red disc of the sun inched past the distant shore of the lake, warm rays cutting across the frigid waters drew wisps of vapor. Steam swirled in tiny vapor puffs lasting for just a moment before dissipating into nothingness...Paul spoke much the same in 2 Corinthians 5:10 when he wrote of the upcoming appointment we all have to stand before Christ's Bema seat. Paul used the word *phaulon* for "bad". Such a colorful word used by Greeks for the dust whipped up by the gust of wind on a dirty street. Also used of steam swirls on a boiling pot of water, it describes exactly what I saw that early morning so long ago. Although the wispy trails swirled, ascended and formed fabulous shapes, they all became nothingness in a second. That is the last word of 2 Corinthians 5:10.

Titus 2 is a list of five things for older women that are "good," and seven things for younger women that are "good." And if your life is characterized by these twelve things, you will, at the end of your life, get to the judgment seat of Christ, and instead of finding you spent your life on things that were phaulon, good for nothing, things that were pleasant and not sin, but that in eternity vanish away into nothingness and ashes, you will find eternal rewards.

In English, this fourth characteristic, "teachers of good things," is four words, but in Greek, it's just one: *kalodidaskalous.* "Good things teaching." It's a person whose life is characterized by teaching good things. Their life is a constant teaching lesson of what God says is good. That makes this single word very powerful. This life is an example, a model, a giant billboard advertising what God says is good.

This word explains to us how to keep from suffering loss at Christ's judgment seat. When all our life is passing before Him, and He is examining each of our works to see what is good and what is good for nothing. What's worthless, what's not good, what's not done for Him, will burn up, but what's good will last forever. Our lives are to be living examples to other people of how to live for what is good. How to receive Christ's "well done."

This word describes teaching from example, and together with the last word in the list for older women, speaks of confronting those who don't know what God expects, or don't know that what they're doing doesn't match up with what God desires, and either by example, "teachers of good things," or "admonishing," coming alongside and helping someone stop that and start this, those two things together change the direction of a life, and then a family, and then an entire culture.

How do you do that? This word, *kalodidaskalous,* is not about picking at other people and constantly telling them what they're doing wrong. It's about living your life in such a way that they see it, and wonder about it, and they see in you something they want to imitate.

And here are twelve things God has put His seal of approval on:

1. Reverent behavior, living holy in an unholy world as God's representative.
2. Speech that's under control, speaking gracefully in a graceless world as the oracle of God.
3. Appetites that are under control, having self-discipline in an undisciplined world, not enslaved to anything but Christ.
4. Visible integrity, modeling godliness in a godless world by practicing what you preach, with actions that speak louder than words.
5. Admonishing, investing in others in a detached world.
6. Love for husbands, cultivating a self-sacrificing love in a selfish world.
7. Love for children, cultivating nurturing love in a loveless world.
8. Discretion, focusing on God in a foolish world.
9. Chaste dress and behavior, pursuing modesty in an immodest world.
10. Homemaking, making a home in a hostile world by making every menial task an offering of worship to God.
11. Goodness, pursing kindness in a harsh world.
12. Obedience to husbands, pursing submission in a rebellious world.

Can it really be that simple? Can we really find everything we need in this passage to know what God desires and expects from our lives so that we can live confidently? Can we really know what will matter at the judgment seat of Christ? Is it really that simple? Yes. It is.

When these twelve things are placed, by our choices, into our life, and when they rise before God, coming into His presence, these are twelve things He has said will go straight into the "keep" pile. And as these twelve things are piling up, so are our eternal rewards. And by cultivating these twelve godly characteristics, by putting these things into her cart, by avoiding the things God says are only suitable for burning, the Titus 2 woman's life becomes an example that others begin to follow.

This fourth quality of a godly older woman is visible integrity. I remember when I was in seminary, they used to tell us, "Don't try to live up to your preaching. Preach what you're living." Deal with your own life while you're going through the text. That's a Titus 2 woman. She speaks what she's living. She lives what she's teaching. In 1 Timothy 4:16, Paul tells Timothy to pay close attention to himself first, and then to his teaching. What comes first in God's sight? Your lifestyle, your behavior. And then your teaching. It doesn't matter how great your teaching, how long your doctrinal statement if your life denies everything that you say you believe.

Titus 2 women are show-and-tellers, and they train others in the pattern they have learned. Their walk speaks louder than their talk. Their life is daily placed under God's control in all areas: their tongues, their appetites, and their habits. They do not overindulge themselves, they are not pleasure hungry, and they are not malicious talkers. Their life lived is a lesson to be watched.

A godly woman teaches by her life what is good in God's sight. She carefully chooses the better part as Mary did over Martha. Titus 2 women see every area of their lives as an open book that should and does teach Christ's gracious Lordship. They can say as Paul did in 1 Corinthians 11:1, "Imitate me, just as I also imitate Christ."

Paul, the chiefest of sinners, could say to the Corinthians, "Imitate me." Why? Because, yes, he was imperfect, but he was older in the faith than they were, and he had made those mistakes and been where they were and he had learned what was pleasing to God and he could show them.

By the way, what is an "older" woman? Traditionally, it's someone past raising their children. A younger woman's realm of influence is in her home, but after her children are grown and gone, she moves outside the home into the homes of younger women to teach them how to please God as she already learned to do. For every woman in the church, there is someone older than her who has something to teach her, and there is someone younger than her that she can begin to pour into. Sometimes we think we need a PhD before we can do anything, but that's not God's plan. As soon as you are older than someone, you can turn to them and begin to share and, by the Spirit of God, invest in them.

The Incredible Impact of Godly Older Women

Remember the sin-warped, sin-scarred, mixed up people on the isle of Crete? This was God's plan to reach them. To change them. To change an entire culture.

God instructed the godly older women of the church to seek out a younger woman and to spend time with her and to teach her by example how to change her attitude, how to change her marriage, how to change her family, and how to change her life. This is God's simple plan to make every life count.

It's written down what is good and what is not. But what most people need is a good, wise, exemplary older person who has already yielded their life to God's plan, and who can show them how to do the same. And what happens when God's plan for the Church is put into practice? What are the results of Titus 2 men and women?

At the judgment seat of Christ, Titus 2 men and women will not be ashamed. Think about it. Do you know why God wipes away all tears in heaven? I believe it's because, as Paul says in 2 Corinthians 5:10, that there will be believers, blood-bought, eternally secure believers, who are going to suffer incredible loss at the judgment seat of Christ. Their lives are going to amount to little more than a pile of ash, and they will be, as Revelation 3:18 says, naked and ashamed. Titus 2 men and women, who spend their lives investing in what is good, will not suffer loss at the judgment seat of Christ.

So what are these godly older women supposed to teach? Remember that the model of Titus 2 is practical and not theoretical. The purpose is not to fill their minds with information, but to transform their lives with the practical, hands-on grace of God flowing out in their everyday words and actions.

And what is the first thing that godly older women teach? "To love their husbands."[25] Did you know there are a lot of husbands who don't feel loved by their wives? They know they love them. They know they're committed to them. They know they're godly women. They just don't *feel* loved by their wives.

When the Holy Spirit designed a plan to change the culture, He inspired Paul to write this first: to teach younger women to love their husbands. This changes everything. God wants younger women to cultivate self-sacrificing, friendship love toward their husbands. Why? Because it gets their attention. They see that you are no longer living only for yourself, and that you're purposefully putting them and their needs ahead of your own, and they want to know why. What changed?

It's not an accident that this is first. The Holy Spirit ordered the Bible. And what was the first priority that young married believing women needed to be trained in? To love their husbands. The Holy Spirit believed that the priority to make the New Testament Church the vibrant, holy, spirit-led assembly it became was to start with the newly married women, and get in those homes and train them how to love their husbands.

Can you imagine what a deep and lasting impact upon Christ's Church to have men coming home to a wife who's earnestly being taught to love her own husband? Titus 2 women would encourage a grateful army of husbands who feel deeply loved by their wives. Such a love is a powerful testimony in a culture where women are being pressed into being self-seeking, independent, do-their-own-thing women. Every family would be enriched if every younger woman was taught in a practical, simple, and personal way how to love her own husband. How to focus her life, her love, and her desire on that one that God gave her.

Next, Titus 2 women train younger women in one of the hardest and most rewarding investments in life. It trains them to have children who feel deeply loved by their mothers. An older mother who has already raised her children has wisdom from learning from her own mistakes and failures to actually train a younger mother. The Holy Spirit emphasizes very clearly that the key to raising children is loving them.

---

25   Titus 2:4

Titus 2 women train, teach, model and mentor moms to love their children in ways that can be felt. Studies of our culture tell us one of the most common complaints of the twenty-first-century child is they don't feel loved. Now maybe they are hard to love and maybe they don't stay around long enough to feel it. Most mothers love their children, but many children are not feeling that love. And so Titus 2 women are mentors and tutors that show moms how to love their children in ways that can be felt.

Next, Titus 2 women train younger women in the holiness and purity that pleases God and unleashes the power of the Holy Spirit. There is much suppression of the Spirit of God in our lives when areas of our lives grieve and quench Him. A godly older woman teaches a younger woman how to be discreet, sensible, and wise in her choices. God directs older women to sit with younger women and discuss what pleases Him in a woman's dress, in her behavior, in her conduct.

What a rich resource in churches and lives to have a young woman walking through life side-by-side with a godly, Spirit-filled woman who will daily, lovingly coach and cheer her on in skillful living, as a wife, as a mother, and as a woman of God. This is how we learn, when we can ask why, how, where does God say that? Stop, what did you mean by that? You can't do that in a group setting, but these things are best taught woman to woman, and that's God's design.

A young woman is taught the centrality and priority in God's plan of the home. Homemaking, God says, is to be her priority. Four of the seven things she's supposed to do center around her home. Homemaking is a learned art, and so many women never have the training in what it means to have a godly home. Homemaking is an art that is to be taught and learned and practiced in every Christian home.

A Christian home in a pagan culture was a radically new thing. The skeptical Greco-Roman world could listen all day long to speeches, and they did, but they could not resist a genuine, radically transformed element of everyday life—the family. If they saw these transformed marriages and homes, they would be stunned and start to question.

Can you imagine, in a dark world, how bright a godly marriage would be? In a world where women were little more than servants?

Where husbands' needs were filled elsewhere, can you imagine what it would look like to have a Christian home where the husband couldn't wait to get home to his wife? Can you imagine what that woman would look like to those who saw her? Earnestly seeking to love her husband like a best friend, nurturing and loving her children in a world so incredibly harsh and hostile to the plan God has for the home?

Why should we live this way? "That the word of God may not be blasphemed."[26] When our lives aren't this way, when wives don't love their husbands, when they don't love their children, when they're not discreet, chaste, obedient homemakers, then the world looks at us and sees that we are no different from them, and they blaspheme the God we say we serve. But when our lives, our marriages, our families, our churches stand out against an increasingly dark world, then that's something they can't condemn us for, "that one who is an opponent may be ashamed, having nothing evil to say of you."[27]

Because of God's plan, the church grew out from Crete into a potent force for changing the world. This is the force that "turned the world upside down"[28] that no one could overlook or ignore. They could hate it, they could persecute it, they could reject it, but they couldn't ignore it. They couldn't overlook the grace of God that changed lives and whole families from the inside out.

Like Daniel, and like Joseph, who both stood before the world-ruler of their day with a power that had kings scratching their heads, the Titus 2 woman is someone who stands out as different in her culture, who will have people wondering where her joy and hope and grace comes from, and who, like Daniel and Joseph, can point the world around her to God.

This is God's plan for changing the culture. This is the impact of a woman of grace. And this is the woman who will hear "well done, good and faithful servant," and will have many others hearing the same thing because of her example. Let us pray that our lives will be spent in doing what is eternally useful to God.

26   Titus 2:5
27   Titus 2:8
28   Acts 17:6

God, I thank You for Your plan to conquer the pagan, Roman world back then one life at a time. As the grace of God that brings salvation teaches individuals to deny ungodliness and worldly lusts, to live soberly, righteously, and godly in everyday life. And as they learned that they would turn to someone who wasn't quite as far down the road, and they'd show them what the Lord has taught them. And that swept the ancient world, and the early church was a living family of older serving younger. I pray that that's what You would do in our midst more and more as we see the day of Your return approaching.

Respond to Truth

Many Christians believe God's expressed desires for women in the first century do not apply to the twenty-first-century woman because of the difference in culture. How has the culture changed since first-century Crete?

What level of spiritual maturity do you have to reach before you can start becoming a Titus 2 woman of grace? (See Titus 2:12.)

How does God qualify what is worth doing (2 Corinthians 5:9–10)? How do you qualify what is worth doing? What is the result if what you value doesn't line up with what God values (1 Corinthians 3:13–15)?

How do we know what is good and what is not according to God (2 Timothy 3:16–17)?

Why did Jesus sacrifice Himself for you (Titus 2:11–14)? How should that change your priorities (2 Corinthians 5:14–15)?

God's Call to Sensible Living | 6

On April 10th, 1912, as the greatest, fastest, largest, and most expensive ship in the world docked at Southampton in England, my grandmother held a third-class, lowest-deck ticket to the maiden voyage of the *Titanic*.

But as she stood in line at the White Star Line's office, she had to get a refund. As she sought to board the boat, she was turned away at the gangplank because her passport papers from the embassy, which had gone through, had something missing. The clerk had failed to stamp one small area of her paperwork, so on the gangway, she was denied boarding.

As the blast of the departure horn sounded, my grandmother was handed tickets for another ship, the TSS *Rotterdam*. She would sail, again third class, on another day so she could go back after the weekend to have her paperwork stamped and signed.

We all know the story of what happened four days later. The *Titanic* plummeted to its watery grave two miles beneath the icy waters of the north Atlantic. For me, I've always been amazed at God's providence, because if that clerk hadn't missed that small area on my grandmother's paperwork, if my grandmother had gotten on board, my mother would never have been born in 1920, nor me in 1956, nor any of our eight children since 1985. Think about how amazing God's providential hand is.

From that event, the tragic sinking of the *Titanic* in 1912, there came a saying. When it's nice what someone's doing, but they're missing something huge going on around them, we compare it to arranging or stacking the deck chairs on the *Titanic*. Something monumentally important is going on, but they're just piddling around with something little.

So with that scene on your mind, I want you to look at Titus 2. Paul captures this idea, of getting someone's attention and refocusing it, to urgently making them see that we are called to something so much greater than us, so much bigger than anything else we could find to do. And God calls for the godly older women of the church to see those around them who are busily stacking the deck chairs and to help them come to their senses.

Titus 2:3–4. "The older women, likewise, that they be reverent in behavior, not slanderers, not given to much wine, teachers of good things— that they admonish."

To Call to One's Senses

As we come to the last quality for older women in Titus 2, this is the quality that all the others are building to. She is not merely to be the one who has the character God desires, but there's one more quality, that she "admonish." The word is *sophron* or *sophronidzus,* and it means that she goes through life calling people to their senses.

Sophronidzus, translated into English as "that they admonish," or "discreet," or "sensible," or "self-controlled," is really a huge word in secular literature. The New Testament was written in Koine Greek, and there's a huge body of Koine Greek literature from the Roman Empire from the time of the church. Many times the words of the Bible are used all over the place out in everyday life, and I have huge books in my library that chronicle the use of Biblical words in secular settings. And here is how this word, that God had Paul choose, was used in everyday Greek life in the first century:

Sophron means to not be known as a clown. They had jesters and clowns back then, and the *sophron* person was never clowning around. Also, to be serious in life, or to be serious about spiritual things.

Sophron also referred to living a disciplined, self-controlled, un-addicted-to-anything life. In meant to be in control of your choices, to avoid excesses.

Sophron spoke of knowing your priorities and having clear thoughts that led to an orderly life.

All of that is part of what God wants. What God is saying in this verse is that we should get serious about what He wants, and to reach out into the lives of others and lovingly come alongside them to ask if they've ever thought about what God wants, if they're serious about those things, and to encourage them to make Him their priority.

The God of the universe loves you so much He sent His Son to die for you, in your place, on the cross, for your sin. Do you realize that's just the beginning of all He wants for you? Such love He offers to you constrains you to respond and give yourself back to Him. Have you thought about that?

The Greeks looked at this word *sophron* or *sophronedzus* as having a life that was constrained or restrained or bounded by a set of ideals, and in the case of Titus 2, those ideals would be the words of God. And that word got taken by the Apostle Paul, by the inspiration of the Spirit, to be used for a life that is constrained by God's desires. My life is to be built around God's desires, not mine.

This is the only universal quality in Titus 2 that God wants for every person in His church. It's in every list, for the older men, the older women, the younger women, and the younger men. This is the quality God desires as part of the life of faith for every believer's life.

Starting in verse 2: "that the older men be sober, reverent, temperate." "Temperate" is the word *sophron*, the word for coming to your senses, of living a life restrained by a set of ideals, a life built around God's desires.

Next one, verse 4: "that they admonish," and that's the one we're looking at, that the godly older women aren't just to be sensible and living according to God's desires, but they have a lifestyle of calling others to that same high calling, of bringing others to their senses. And what is it that they're supposed to train the younger women to do?

Verse 5: "to be discreet." Whatever word you have in your version of the Bible, it's the same word, that the older women are to call the younger women to have this life that is sensible and serious about spiritual things, constrained again by God's ideals.

And the younger men aren't left out. Look at verse 6: "Likewise, exhort the young men to be sober-minded." *Sophronos,* the very first quality on the list for younger men.

What is the one word that sums up the only spiritual quality that God personally asked to be taught to everyone in Christ's Church? What is the one word that sums up the first lifestyle choice every young man who wants to mature his heart in God's Word should have? What is the one word that sums up the ministry of every older woman of grace who has allowed God to shape her heart's desires? What is the one word that sums up the characteristic shared by every older man and every younger woman of the Church?

It's *sophron,* this life constrained by God's desires. I exchange my desires for His. I am called to my senses by God. I am admonished to live a life God's way. I have the universal quality that God has commanded all of us to have, of calling people to respond to God. Not to follow us, but to follow us like we're following God. And then we can slide out of the way, and they begin following God themselves.

God commands us to spend our lives investing in the lives of other people showing them how they can follow Jesus like we do. This means, in the context of "that they admonish" of verse 4, that a mature older believer wants to be personally investing in others in their life.

Look at verse 12. "We should live soberly." *Sophron.* God wants us serious about spiritual things and restoring others to serious spiritual living. So verse 4 coupled with verse 12 tells us God is looking for godly, mature women who will make it their lifelong goal to resist the temptations of self-absorption.

Most of us know what God wants, but we just sit there like the parking brake is on. Verse 12 tells us how we get unstuck. God's grace has appeared, bringing salvation, "teaching us that, denying ungodliness and worldly lusts, we should live" *sophron,* "soberly, righteously, and godly." What is the key to making us live soberly? The grace of God that brings salvation. God's grace empowers us, if we want to obey Him, to reach into other people's lives. That's what I call grace-energized living.

We live in a detached world where we don't often break out of our little group of people we're comfortable with. God says we are to break out of that comfort zone and start investing in others. And we actually say to them, "I used to waste my life. And I didn't realize that God had a calling for me to be reverent in my behavior. And I didn't realize that everything I said mattered to Him, and I didn't realize that all my appetites were to be under His command. And I want you to understand that because You belong to Him too."

We live every day surrounded by doomed people. They're not even aware of the judgment for sin they'll eternally face. And if we're not careful to reach out and touch others' lives with God's Word, all that we do in life is no more valuable than arranging chairs on a sinking ship. The measure of our life is whether what we're doing is useful to God.

If you were on that ship all those years ago and saw one of your dearest friends, completely oblivious to the disaster that was coming upon then, busily stacking the lounges and straightening the chairs, just think how clear your feeling of responsibility would be toward them. If you saw the ship was sinking and they didn't, wouldn't you want to look that person in the eyes and say, "what you're doing is wonderful. It's helpful. But what you don't understand is that you're investing all your efforts on a sinking ship. Focus your efforts on what you're supposed to be doing. Get yourself and as many people as you can off this doomed boat."

Can you understand the urgency you would feel? If they were your friend, would you just walk on by them and let them be unprepared for what was coming? The deck is shuddering, the ship is sinking, and someone you know, you love, you care about is just busily stacking the deck chairs, oblivious to what's going on around them. You would feel obligated, responsible, to immediately get their attention, to call them to their senses, to point out the tilt of the ship, the iceberg floating out there, and urge them to get to the lifeboats.

That's the idea of *sophronedzus*. That passion is what Paul's trying to communicate. We have been saved from doom. The One who saved us left us to live a life that is useful to Him. And to be useful to Him, we have to get in step with the plan that He left in His word. And so the whole goal of life is not just making it, but staying in step with the plan. And because we realize that we have been left on earth to please God, and because we realize that we are living life on a sinking ship, we begin to get in step with God's plan.

Now you may be getting a little queasy, not sure you want to walk up to someone and tell them they're wasting their life. They might point out all the ways you're wasting yours. But we are to go to them, our friends who are wasting their lives doing what does not please God, and, after we have examined our own life, we reach out to the lives of those around us and say, "Don't waste your precious life."

We don't just observe others. As believers, we step out of our comfort zone and say, "I used to spend endless hours doing that, but let me tell you what God says counts forever, and it's changed my life, and maybe you should consider that in your agenda, your priorities." That would be an example of calling the deck-chair-arrangers to their senses.

Paul uses the word *paramutheo* for this idea. To pull someone aside and whisper in their ear. And you say, "this is empty, and this will not last, and you will waste your life if you keep going this way." And there is no greater priority for a woman of grace than this.

Investing in Others in a Detached World

Do you know why the Titus 2 woman is so powerful in the Church? Because everything she does, every quality she cultivates in her life as an older woman is geared toward and directed toward being this godly mentor who can admonish a younger woman in what pleases God.

Remember, she lives like a holy priest, serving in the presence of God. Her sacred, personal devotion to the Lord slowly influences and controls every part of her life. She does not allow herself, Romans 12:2, to be conformed to the world, but she is progressively being transformed by the renewing of her mind. This is why she is so powerful in the Church, because she can help younger women see areas in their lives where they have been conforming to the world.

Remember what "reverent in behavior" meant? It means that this godly older woman is a living temple of God. Why? What was a temple for? It was the place people would come to see their god. And Paul says we are the photographs of Christ, the image of Christ. You and I are the representation of Christ. He's written in our hearts. We are living letters from Christ. We demonstrate Christ. That's what we are to be. He's living in us, and living out through us, and people see and are drawn to that. This godly older woman isn't reverent in her behavior just so her own life can be right with God. She's reverent and lives as a temple to lead other people into the presence of God, namely that younger woman that she is earnestly mentoring.

Do you remember why Paul warned Timothy and Titus about the dangers of gossip and slander? Because, especially for this godly older woman, the control she has over her tongue either qualifies her or disqualifies her for this ministry. If her tongue is out of control, if she's a gossip, how can she have this close, intimate, nurturing relationship with a younger woman who is just learning how to love her husband and children and be discreet and chaste and obedient? How can she cultivate the trust she needs if that younger woman knows anything she tells that older woman is just going to be told at the next house she goes to?

Why is it so important for a godly older woman to be a model of what is good? When Paul or Titus would preach, they would put out there this great truth, and it was just hanging out there. And those early believers heard those truths. They actually heard Paul, in person. And they would go, "Wow." But as soon as the sermon was over, they had to go back to making chariots, or trampling out grapes in the vineyard. And they couldn't connect the wonderful truth they heard to where they were and how they could live that out.

Remember, in the ancient world, marriage was a convenience for legitimate heirs and to have someone you trust watching over your home. Men found their companionship, their emotional intimacy, and their physical intimacy outside of marriage. So when they got saved, they didn't immediately know how to express genuine love to their wives. So Titus gets up and he's reading this letter from Paul, and he reads that younger women are to love their husbands, but how? How do you love this man who maybe is still unsaved and still treating you like a slave and still emotionally distant from you? How do you love him the way Christ wants wives to love their husbands? They needed a model, a living example of someone who has already learned how to love her husband and knows practical, hands-on ways to cultivate the kind of love Titus 2 talks about.

In a way that Paul or Titus or any other pastor of a church can't do, the godly older woman can come and say, "I was in a marriage like yours, and I had a husband like you have, and he was insensitive and uncaring and unthinking, and even though he came to Christ he didn't know how to relate to me. And I'll show you how I became his best friend." And the commands of the Scripture would come alive when a younger woman could see someone actively living out what the Scripture says.

I think sometimes we forget what God intended. We have all our devices and we can listen to God's word in our cars, but God never intended for someone who couldn't see you, who didn't know you, to be all you listen to and then you sort out what you want and what you don't want. Back then, they had a living person who came alongside them and said, "You have been crucified with Christ. You are dead to this. There should be a decreasing frequency of anger in your life. A decreasing frequency of impatience. The fruit of the Spirit should be evident in your life, and there can be growing joy in your life."

What would you think if you had someone sitting next to you right now, saying that to you? Can you imagine? You'd look at them and say, "Really?" And they'd say, "Just now, the way you responded to your husband. That's not loving." "Really?" Can you imagine how fast people grew like that? This person's around them, they see them regularly. That was the ministry of these Titus 2 women in the early church.

Christ's Church grew in the first century into that potent force that changed the world in the quiet, nurturing sessions of Titus 2. That's what's so amazing. They just lived those 33 Greek words of the Titus 2 passage. And they did quiet, nurturing sessions, and practical discipleship. And just as important as the preaching and teaching of the doctrines of God's Word was the modeling and nurturing of individual believers through the practical, hands-on lessons these women performed.

Titus 2 women were not primarily found in the classroom. They were in the kitchens with a younger woman, in the dining room, in the nursery, at the grocery store. They were hands-on tutors nurturing younger women in the laboratory of life, walking through life together, praying, sharing, learning, and loving.

Titus 2:12, the goal of every man, woman, and child in the Church, is to live "soberly," *sophron,* "righteously and godly." That's the truth that we hear from the pulpit. But then, all of these qualities, all twelve of them, are how we live that out in everyday life. They're just the specifics of what God has told us to do in Titus 2:12.

For a believing marriage partner, this quality of *sophron,* learned as a young person, leads to a heart attitude of mutual submission. Do you see how important it is to teach this to young people? If they can learn this when they're young, they will have a godly, love-prompted marriage and home. Every building block of a godly marriage and home, including a self-sacrificing spirit and a loving and tender tongue and a compassionate heart flow from a person saying, "God, I want to build my life around Your ideals. Your Word." *Sophron* is choosing to let my life be built around God's priorities, and then realizing that one of His priorities is that I don't just build my life around it, but I help others. I actually reach out to them and lovingly tell them to quit stacking those chairs, because the boat's sinking.

Paul did teach in churches, but no matter where he was or what he was doing or what letters he was writing, he always had a Titus, he always had a Timothy, an Epaphroditus, an Onesimus, that he was pouring into and mentoring and leading along and maturing. Every older believer, whether it's a man with younger men, or a woman with younger women, is called to admonish someone else in the faith, to devote their lives, to open their homes, to invest their time to pour into another person in God's church.

God is looking for men and women who will mentor, who will nurture, who will coach godly living for His Church. These individuals know that God has called them to touch one life at a time for His glory. Today, we like to do mass marketing, big events. That's not what God describes here. The early church was nurturing individuals.

In the early church as God designed it, it was the highest desire of each man and woman to pour their lives into another individual, and when they got done pouring into that person, they went and poured into another person. God deployed the godly older women of the Church to intentionally seek out and mentor every younger woman in the Church and pour into them. And when God got to pick the curriculum, when He got to design the lesson plan, He picked twelve godly character qualities that every man should have, and twelve vital character qualities for every woman of grace.

Women who want to be useful to God seek to master these twelve character qualities so that they can admonish a younger woman in the last seven. Parents who want their children to be useful to God point them from the earliest age to becoming a Titus 2 man or woman. And the highest priority of a godly older woman, what every other quality she's mastered has been preparing her for, is to train younger women in biblical, practical, simple-to-measure, Spirit-empowered, love-based living. She aspires to the high calling and great joy of entering the home and life of another woman and pouring her love, her life, and most of all her godly experience into that younger woman's life and marriage and family.

That They Admonish

Women energized by grace are earnest mentors. In the KJV, they "teach," in the NKJ, they "admonish," NIV, they "train," NASB, they "encourage." But what's their lesson plan? What does this admonishing, encouraging ministry look like?

If I were a godly older woman, this is how I'd apply this. If I were in a Bible study, I would say to the young woman I was meeting with, "Did you know God has seven desires, God personally, for you and your life?"

And she would look at me and say, "Where?" So I'd have her open her Bible, and if she didn't have one, I'd open mine and show her where, verse 4 of Titus 2, I'm supposed to admonish her, I'm supposed to encourage her, I'm supposed to call her to her senses on these seven qualities:

"To love their husbands, to love their children, to be discreet, chaste, homemakers, good, obedient to their own husbands."[29]

And do you know what I'd tell her? If you're married, or are ever going to be married, God wants you to love your husband. But whether or not

---

29   Titus 2:4–5

you're ever married, the God of the universe is pleased by your life if you cultivate a self-sacrificing love, because you live in a selfish world.

Do you know what this is all about? This is not about getting married or not getting married. This "loving the husbands" is a much larger thing than just being isolated to a ring on your finger. It's a lifestyle of self-sacrificing love in the face of selfishness. Only the grace of God can prompt that. So I'd point her to where God says that in verse 12. And we'd talk about that for a while.

And the next time we got together, I'd take her to the second quality in verse 4, "to love their children." If you're married and have children, God wants you to love your children. Now if it's a nine-year-old girl looking at me across the table, she doesn't have any children. But I'd say to her that even if she's never married or never has children, the God of the universe will be pleased by her life if she cultivates nurturing love in a loveless world.

In the first century, they were loveless. They didn't have nurturing love. That's why Paul had to command that women be trained to love their children. But this is not about Parenting 101. This is a lifestyle change. Nurturing love goes beyond the basics. It doesn't just say to the children, "eat your food." It's a love that nurtures and helps them to grow. And so I would train this young woman in what the God of the universe wants in nurturing love and show her how Christ did that.

Next, "to be discreet." I would say to her that no matter her situation, her background, or her temperament, the God of the universe who owns her wants her to be discreet. What's that? He's pleased when you focus on what God wants from you instead of what a foolish world wants from you. Remember this is *sophron* again, building your life, constraining it around God's ideals, instead of around the passing fancies of the world. That's lesson three.

Lesson four: "chaste." Even in the midst of a society of wickedness, even if everyone else does it, if you want your life to be rewarded with the greatest joy of all, when you hear Christ's "well done, good and faithful servant," then you must obey God's command that you be "chaste." And as she looked and said, "what does that word mean?" I would begin a lesson explaining that Jesus Christ is pleased when He sees you pursuing modesty in an immodest world.

The world of Paul's day is the world we see captured in all the statues of the Greco-Roman world. Most of them have next-to-nothing on. That was the culture of the day. It'd be like watching today's movies two thousand years from now. They'd catch what our world is like, frenzied, demonized, and immoral. That's what their statues portray to us.

And so I would say the fourth lesson is to pursue modesty. But then we'd get to the next one, "homemakers," and can you imagine my nine-year-old or twelve- or sixteen-year-old sitting across from me when I say, "lesson five is that you become a homemaker." Does that mean doing the dishes? No. If you're married, with or without children, the God who made you desires that you respond to His call and be a homemaker.

The homemaker, the *oikergoi,* the "worker in the house" is tied to marriage, to making a home in marriage. But even if you're never married, and whether or not you ever have children, God still asks you to please Him by pursuing a welcoming home in a hostile world. Do you know what's commanded to all believers? That they be lovers of strangers. That we reach out to people who aren't in our circle and invite them to our home group, our Bible study, our lunch group that meets, and we make a welcoming place in a hostile world. That's lesson number five.

Number six, that they be "good." And the colder and darker the world may get, Jesus wants us standing out as "good" as a contrast to "bad." And specifically, our Master in heaven is pleased when we pursue kindness in a harsh world. Remember how Jesus was described in one of the apostolic sermons? That He went around doing good. Jesus was characterized by being good.

And finally, the last one, "obedient to their own husbands." Finally, for every woman who is married, the Lord has clearly called you to an attitude of submission to your husband. The word means to line up behind or fall into rank. It's the attitude of submitting and lining up behind him. And God says if you're married, He's calling you to an attitude of submission to your husband, but whether or not you're ever married, God is pleased and will reward those who pursue submission in a rebellious world.

The surest way to get someone to do something is to tell them to not do it, and their flesh makes them want to do it. When I teach at camp, I tell my campers, "don't look at what I'm writing on the board," and all of a sudden every eye is glued to me. It's just ingrained inside of us to go against. We live in a rebellious world, and God wants us to go against that nature inside us and to pursue an attitude of submissive obedience.

All these qualities are how we practically live out the command of Titus 2:12 to live "soberly," *sophron* "righteously, and godly." The godly older woman realizes that she lives on a sinking ship. She encourages the younger women to pursue what is worth living for, investing her time, money, and strength carefully, living by priority instead of in the moment, and becoming contented with fewer and simpler things.

She encourages the younger woman not to give in to overindulgence, knowing from God's Word that the pleasures of self-indulgence cost far more than they're worth. She encourages her in mental sobriety, self-restraint, the freedom from debilitating or rash decisions, from rash words, or rash behavior, and encourages her to be stable, circumspect, and clear thinking.

She encourages the younger woman in exercising appropriate priorities, and placing emphasis where God does. She encourages her to be in charge of her priorities, to be steadfast, morally decisive, not under the sway of the allurements of the world, the flesh, and the devil. She encourages her not to be controlled by outside circumstances but directed by inward convictions.

This is God's clearly stated desire for you, that you grow into a woman who can encourage and call to their senses other women, to admonish them. Offer your time, offer your words, open your schedule to them. Don't waste your life arranging the deck chairs of life. They're going to wash away anyway. The world is sinking and generation after generation is passing into eternity covered in their sins and sinking to the depths of eternal punishment. And the most widely-felt impact on our culture is to deploy people who will live His way in culture. And if they will do that, live out His design for Christ's church before a watching world, if they will live a life that conforms to His ideals, then people will be drawn to ask why. And Jesus said by this, by this love you have, your investment in others and desire to conform to His desires, people will know you are His disciples.

Father, how I pray that this word "admonish," this one word that's the only universal quality for everyone in Christ's Church, that this word will become a part of our lives. That we will all come to our senses, and be those who call others to see Your call upon their lives. May we re-consecrate ourselves to live life the way You want us to live it. And not just make sure that we make it in the lifeboat, but that we reach out to others, to other believers who are frittering their lives away, wasting their days, and we tell them what Your plan is and how they can please You with their lives. Let this not be merely theoretical, but may each godly woman seek to enfold a younger woman and become close enough friends to be able to call her to her senses and start pouring her life into that woman. That's our cry. That's our request. Hear us now in the name of Jesus, we pray. Amen.

Respond to Truth

How would people describe you? As someone who behaves as a priest and a temple of God? As someone who would never gossip about anyone else and is safe to bring into their confidence? As someone who could live without absolutely anything as long as she has God? Would they say, "I want to follow God like she does"?

If you were to examine your schedule, your hobbies, your priorities, the list of things you care about, how much of it is going down with a sinking ship? What does grace teach you to do about that (Titus 2:11–14)?

If you are seeking to live soberly, righteously, and godly, what is your responsibility toward your family, your friends, and your brothers and sisters in Christ (Matthew 7:5; Philippians 2:3–4; James 5:19–20)?

What does God say is so vital to a ministry of calling people to their senses that if you lack this, your ministry will be useless (1 Corinthians 13)?

Where do the results in people come from (1 Corinthians 3:5–7)? What does God say rewards are given for (1 Corinthians 3:8)?

7 | Self-Sacrificing Love in a Selfish World

My son gave me his iPhone a few months back, and I was having more fun just piddling around with it, and all of a sudden it didn't work. So I called him up on the other phone and said, "I've done something wrong." He said, "Don't worry, Dad. You can put it right back. You can just restore it." So I did what he said and just hooked the bottom into the computer and it talks to something, some other computer, and it takes a while, and it comes up and tells you it's working. And all of a sudden it was right back in place again. It was reset to the factory settings.

Most marriages are not operating the way that God designed them to operate, but God offers service calls. And He will reset us, any time, back to the original settings. My prayer is that we would get plugged into God's Word, and through prayer and communication with Him, and through seeing what our settings are supposed to be, that we would return to what God says works.

Titus 2:4 is God's call to women to reset their marriages back to the factory settings. When God invented marriage, when He created Adam and formed Eve from Adam, God designed that they be one, in their hearts, their lives, their pathway, their direction, their emotions, that they would have the kind of love described in Titus 2. *Philandrois.* "Husband-lovers." These women are love-filled, respect-reflecting, and the best friend in all the world to their husbands.

So where does love like that come from? Let's go back to the beginning, to the original settings that God designed.

THE FACTORY SETTINGS FOR MARRIAGE

The Bible is under attack. And do you know why the most scoffed-at portion of the Bible is right at the beginning? It's not just that it's the Word of God and Satan likes to undermine anything to do with the Word of God. It's because if God did not create all things, and if God did not design marriage, then we have no absolutes. It's because Genesis 1–2 is where we find the manufacturer's settings, the Creator's settings, for marriage.

By the way, I believe in a six-day literal creation, not because of Genesis 1, but because of Exodus 20. I believe in the full, word-by-word, verbal inspiration of God. The Holy Spirit moved and breathed out through forty different authors the very words of God, except for one place in Exodus 20. This is why I don't give any ground on creation, because this is the one passage in all of Scripture that God actually wrote Himself. It wasn't dictated to godly men and they wrote it down. God actually showed up on a mountain, reached down, and carved these words into stone with His finger.

"For in six days the Lord made the heavens and earth, the sea, and all that is in them, and rested the seventh day. Therefore the Lord blessed the Sabbath day and hallowed it."[30]

Do you know how people understood that back then? You realize these were slaves, just out of Egypt, and God is giving them a list of ten commandments, and number 4, remember the Sabbath day and keep it holy, is explained, by God, this way: you do your work for six days, and then on the seventh day you rest. Why? Because God worked for six days, and on the seventh day He rested.

So, with the very finger of God, we have the whole account of creation written in stone. But in Genesis 2, we go back to where God describes in detail, not just what He made, but how and why He made it.

For a whole chapter, Genesis 1, there's a pattern, a kind of rhythm to what God makes. And on the first day, God did this, and God saw that it was good. And on the second day, God did this, and God saw that it was good. And on and on until we come to day six, and God creates man, and then something changes. For the first time in history God says, "Not good."

Before the fall, before sin, before the warping of the family and of marriage and of personal lives by sin, God found something that was "not good." Everything else was good. But when God made Adam, He said, "This isn't good." What wasn't good? It wasn't good that Adam would be alone. Isn't that amazing? Before there was any sin, any evil, any conflict, any rivalry, there was aloneness, and God described it as not good.

When God finished the rest of His creation, He crowned it with something He made in His own image—a man. But there was something missing. Something unfinished. Something "not good." Literally, "not good is man's aloneness." So God crowns the six days of stellar creation with Eve. The highest point of creation, the pinnacle, made in the image of God, was "not good" without that crowning of creation, Eve.

Adam went and named all the animals. He looked over the whole created world, and there was no one that fit with him, that communed with him, that corresponded to him, that was like him. So God created the first woman, Eve, to be Adam's close and cherished companion, his friend, his completer. That was marriage divine-style, the way it was intended to be.

God's original plan and design for husbands and wives, before the fall, before sin, was for men to be incomplete without their woman, the woman made for them. That's not a defect. That was planned into the design by God. God left out that completer so that it would be found in another, one who was designed just to complete him. And in doing so, God established a vital truth, that a fulfilling, harmonious marriage can only be lived God's way, the way God designed it to be.

There is a wealth of marriage-changing truth in these few words from God. "It is not good that man should be alone; I will make him a helper comparable to him."[31]

The first truth is men need close companionship. Some say that dog is man's best friend, but when Adam looked over all the animal kingdom, he

---

31   Genesis 2:18

did not find the close companionship that he needed. Dog is not man's best friend. Wife is man's best friend.

Aloneness, solitary living, is not good. One of the deepest pains sociologists have measured in society is living an isolated and lonely life. They report that such people ache with a deep pain they can't even fully describe. And God saw that in Adam. He saw his need, and so God did something. He decided to create a "helper."

Now the way we think of the word "helper" today is really not what the Hebrew says at all. Here's how Webster's dictionary defines "helper:" "one who helps, especially a relatively unskilled worker who assists a skilled worker, usually by manual labor." How do you like that? That is what a lot of unsaved people think Christian marriage is, a rather unskilled wife assisting the very skilled husband, like a bricklayer, just handing him the bricks and doing whatever he says.

That's not at all what God said. The word God chose means something grand. Literally it describes a person who assists another to reach complete fulfillment. This is a person who comes alongside another and assists them to reach or achieve or arrive at what they were meant to be and meant to do.

If you want a good way to study the Bible, look at how a word is used in other places in Scripture. So if you were to look up the Hebrew word "helper," you'd find that is used for someone who goes and rescues another person. Think about it. Eve was created to rescue Adam from his "not good aloneness." She was supposed to save him from being alone. And she was supposed to fulfill him in a way he couldn't be fulfilled without her. Eve was to fill a God-designed necessary role that rescued Adam from missing his fulfillment. And in the process of being God's special creation for man, Eve also found her completion and fulfillment

Then God continues with another word that captures even more the beauty of marriage. She was also made to be "comparable to him," or some versions say, "suitable for him." She literally "corresponded" to him.

Have you ever tried to put together a puzzle on a rainy day, and you get the whole thing finished but there are pieces missing? That's what Adam was without Eve. She was made to be the missing piece to Adam's life.

Have you ever wondered why God made Eve out of Adam's rib? He could have spoken her into existence, formed her out of clay, taken an orchid and redesigned it if He wanted to. But he took something from Adam, literally, taking a piece out of him to demonstrate that without her, he had a piece missing. He was incomplete, and God fashioned that rib into woman. To be the missing piece that he was incomplete without.

As the missing piece to Adam's life, Eve was made to correspond to him, to fit him, to be his perfect match, intellectually, emotionally, physically, and spiritually. When God made this promise in verse 18, to make a helper suitable for Adam, He promised to design her exactly to specifications for Adam.

Eve wasn't out there among the animals, and Adam went and found the prettiest animal and grabbed her. That's not what happened. But that's how a lot of people look at marriage. You go out, shop around, and grab one. Find the best one. But that's not how God originally designed marriage to be. We are looking for that one person that God has already designed specifically for us, to complete us on every level. That's what the last part of God's promise is, that she would be "for him."

Can you imagine that moment? Adam woke up from the divine anesthesia, and he saw God coming toward him, and on God's arm was the most beautiful thing Adam had ever seen. And Adam thought, "wow, this is what I searched the whole world for and couldn't find." This was what he had been searching for, what he'd been aching for, what he was incomplete without, his rescuer, his completer, and God was personally bringing her to Adam on His arm, the one He fashioned just for him.

The word "fashioned" means to "build or rebuild so as to cause to flourish." When the missing piece from Adam was taken by God and fashioned, that missing piece of his life's puzzle flourished into Eve. She was his helper, his completer, his satisfier, and the one who fulfilled every dimension of his life as a man.

"And Adam said, 'This is now bone of my bone and flesh of my flesh; she shall be called Woman, because she was taken out of Man.'"[32] When he says, "this is," in Hebrew, it's like it's got an exclamation point on it. It's like

32 Genesis 2:23

he's saying, "This is it! What I've searched the whole world for!" So Adam exclaims that his wife, Eve, was made by God, given to him by God, specially designed, and intentionally made for his needs as he was for hers.

From the start, each partner was unique, each partner was vital, each partner was distinct, and each had a God-designed role that provided immense satisfaction, fulfillment, and completion. Think about it. Eve was made *for* Adam. She was literally made *from* Adam. Eve was brought *to* Adam. And she was named *by* Adam. There was an incredible equality about them. They were both made by God, both made in the image of God, made to complement each other, but not to compete with each other.

Eve's role designed by God was to respond to Adam's initiatives, follow Adam's lead, comfort him as he protected her, receive Adam's provision, and love him in all dimensions as her husband, but something happened. For the first time in human history, husband and wife reversed their roles. Have you ever thought about that? The first time the wife abandoned her role as the helper, she was deceived by Satan, she ate the forbidden fruit, and she led her husband into sin. And Adam. He was supposed to be the spiritual leader, the protector. His role was to initiate, lead, protect, provide, cherish, and husband his wife, but he abandoned his God-given role and followed Eve into sin. And the relationship between a husband and his wife has only been deteriorating ever since.

The further away we get from the original plan, the further away from the creation event we get, and the further away from the Scriptures society gets, the more there is a breakdown of an understanding of what marriage is all about, and of what the husband and wife relationship is.

By the time of Deuteronomy 24, Moses had to make provisions in the Law for divorce, something God never intended, never wanted, but because of the sinfulness of human nature, it was permitted in certain circumstances. But by the time of Christ, those provisions in the Law had been expanded far beyond what God wrote down to include anything a husband didn't like. He could get a divorce at any time, for any reason, if his wife did anything he didn't like. Sound like today? If one of you isn't happy, you file for divorce. Just get out and go be happy somewhere else.

In the Greek culture, women were treated, not as the perfect completion of their husband, but as little more than a servant to be used and cast aside, and a husband would go out and have his sexual and emotional needs met somewhere else. Consorts and concubines were so common that the words adultery and fornication were unheard of. No one expected anything different.

In Roman culture, the idea of a woman being her husband's missing piece was laughable. She was encouraged to go outside the home, to lead a life apart from her husband, to be her own person. Don't let him treat you like a slave. Don't let him make you disappear. Much like in our American culture today, a woman was encouraged to be independent and self-seeking, and these things were treated as virtues.

All three are wrong. They're errors. Marriage was never meant to end in divorce. Wives were never meant to be treated as servants who had to put up with their husbands' abuse and infidelity. And women were never meant to throw off the authority of their husbands and do their own thing. This isn't enlightenment. This is the curse.

The God who doesn't change hated divorce in the Old Testament, hated it in the New Testament, and still hates it today. The God who commanded faithfulness to one's wife by carving it into stone with His own finger also commanded husbands to love their wives as Christ loved the church in Ephesians 5, and still desires a close, loving relationship between a husband and wife today. And the God who commanded wives to be husband-lovers, lovers of children, homemakers, and submissively obedient to their own husbands in Titus 2 has the same expectation for women today.

I lived through the eighties on staff at Grace Community Church in Los Angeles, and John MacArthur preached the pastoral epistles on the role of women. There were 10,000 of us inside the church, and there were hundreds of protesters outside the church. You almost couldn't even make it inside because hundreds of Californians were standing with these great big signs and chanting and protesting and marching back and forth in front of Grace Community Church, simply because John MacArthur dared to preach that God actually has expectations that are gender-specific.

This section of Scripture, where women are called to love their husbands, to love their children, to be obedient to their own husbands, and especially to be homemakers is the single most contested portion of the epistles among the commentators. They want to say this is not for today, that a woman should not be made to believe she should be a homemaker and raise her children, she shouldn't be told that this is God's calling on her life.

But Paul thought that. Titus thought that. The New Testament church thought that. But not because of their culture. In spite of it. They believed this was God's call for them, and because God's word hasn't changed, and because the God who wrote it hasn't changed, we believe that this is God's call for all godly women who wish to do marriage God's way.

This is not optional. It's not like these are the optimum settings for the best marriage possible, but if you want to do things another way, that's fine. No. If you are not this kind of wife, a love-filled, respect-reflecting, best-friend-in-all-the-world to your husband, then you are disobeying God. It's not a choice between being this kind of wife and being a different kind of wife. It's a choice between pleasing God and living in direct disobedience to Him.

As in today's culture, by the time Titus 2 was written, women loving their own husbands was a revolutionary concept. But in obedience to God, these women chose to live this way in spite of their lack of experience—they'd never done this before. They chose to love their husbands in spite of lack of example—they'd never seen this done before. In fact, they didn't even know of any other church that was living this way. This was the first time it was ever taught, this love-filled, respect-reflecting, best-friend-in-all-the-world lifestyle. But godly younger women chose to be obedient to God and learn, from those older in the faith who were also learning this for the first time, to become what Paul calls in Titus 2 "husband-lovers."

The Revolutionary Concept of Husband-Lovers

Imagine with me for a moment as this letter, the letter to Titus, made its way to the congregation on Crete. This letter came from the most recognized, the most admired and respected, and the most authoritative representative of God on the planet, the Apostle Paul. This wasn't just any letter. It was special delivery, couriered directly to this island and handed to Pastor Titus.

So as Titus broke the seal on the letter Paul had written, imagine the excitement of the congregation. And as Titus gets up and reads chapter 1, they hear about their great salvation and transformation, then he gets to chapter 2, and they hear that because of the grace of God, because of that salvation, God wants them to live a certain way. So as Titus gets to chapter 2, you know each member of the congregation had to sit up a little straighter. And as their categories were called one by one, they waited expectantly to find out what God wanted, specifically, individually, from them.

So he reads about the older men, and that was pretty standard. Then the older women, and that was pretty expected. But as he comes to verse 4 and reads God's first expectation for the younger women of the church, there had to be shock going through the congregation. The God of the universe wanted them to love—this guy? The man sitting next to them? This husband who didn't understand them and didn't know how to relate to them and who was insensitive?

I imagine many of the husbands leaned over and said, "did he just say what I think he said?" And the women would have very soberly replied, "he did."

Love-Filled

The word is *philandrois*, "husband-lovers." That they "love their husbands," or literally, "love their own man." What a shock. The idea that a Christian home, that a Christian family, was first and foremost to be characterized by a wife who was a "husband-lover" was revolutionary. This went totally contrary to the culture, to the generational models, to all they'd ever heard, seen or read.

We've all heard of *agape* love. We know the love chapter, 1 Corinthians 13. We have *agape* coffee shops, we have *agape* Bible covers, we have *agape* everything. By the time they got this letter, the believers on Crete already knew they were supposed to *agape* each other. This is the word used for loving your enemies, loving your neighbors, and loving fellow believers. But it's not a feeling. It's an action. We are called to act in a loving way toward each other, toward our saved and unsaved friends, and even our enemies. We are to act. We are to do deeds that are prompted by love.

We are never called in the Bible to feel love for our enemies. When someone's spitting on you or hitting you or persecuting you, are you supposed to feel this overwhelming rush of emotions and wish you could spend all your time with them? No. And that is not how we're supposed to love our neighbors. The *agape* love for our neighbors is an action, not an emotion. You may not feel this incredible closeness to them, but when their trash dumps over in your yard, you pick it up for them. That's the self-sacrificial *agape* love.

The love of self-sacrifice was already supposed to be present in marriages. That's the word Paul uses in Ephesians 5:25 and Colossians 3:19 for a husband acting toward his wife in the same self-sacrificing way that Christ loved the church. Women have already been commanded to act in obedient submission with respect to their own husbands in Ephesians 5:22 and Colossians 3:18. Peter adds that women are to cultivate a gentle and quiet spirit that is precious in the sight of God and immensely valuable in marriage.[33] This was a reciprocal relationship of a godly marriage on a behavioral level. The commanded attitude and behavior of believers in marriage is foundational. But that's not the word Paul uses in Titus 2.

The word Paul chooses to use, that every older woman and younger woman in the congregation would have immediately understood, was the deep, emotional love of friendship. *Phileo* is the word for being best friends. It speaks of a love-filled, respect-reflecting, best-friend-in-all-the-world relationship that must have looked impossible to the congregation on Crete.

But how? They'd never done this before. They'd never seen this before. They'd never even heard about this before. But in spite of lack of experience, lack of example, and lack of awareness of this even going on in other churches, God calls women of grace to become "husband-lovers."

Phileo is not a Spirit-prompted proper action. It is an emotional love, a feeling love. It is an emotional longing and friendship on a personal level with a dearest friend. The loving actions of *agape* love can be commanded. Love your enemies, turn the other cheek, don't revile them when they revile

---

33   1 Peter 3:4

you, go the extra mile. That can be commanded. But the emotional *phileo* love is something that has to be learned. It has to be taught, cultivated, practiced, and it takes time. And Paul is telling us that women who do not love their husbands in a way they can feel are disobeying God.

You can tell someone what to do, but you can't tell someone how to feel. It's impossible, to just decide to feel a certain way toward someone. Among Bible-believing women of the first century, it was a big challenge to feel love for their husbands. For various reasons and to various degrees, those women found themselves with little to no feelings of love toward their husbands. They weren't raised to feel love toward their husbands. The culture didn't promote feelings of love toward your husband. And the men's behavior didn't prompt feelings of love. So even though they were saved, they didn't feel love toward their husbands.

Those believing wives of the early church, like those today, almost always wanted to obey the Lord, thus they submitted, they obeyed, they fulfilled their responsibilities to their husbands, but often only dutifully, not lovingly. But think about this: it's not just that loving your husband is a virtue. Paul says not loving your husband in a way he can feel is a sin.

Phileo love is love that is completely devoted to another person. Some women say their husbands are no longer lovable, but having that attitude is disobedience to the clear Word of God. You may not always feel that rush of emotions that characterized your relationship at the beginning of your marriage, but *phileo* goes beyond emotions to a deep contentedness, a level of friendship that is deep, enduring, and satisfying.

And so, women who want to obey God make it their choice, they decide with their minds to follow God's desires for their marriage. To surrender with their will to becoming their husbands' best friends. To intentionally examine their lives for how they can love their husbands in a way that can be felt.

Respect-Reflecting

Romantic love really didn't exist in the Greco-Roman world, at least not between a husband and a wife. Emotional love, psychological needs, and sexual desires were all found outside of marriage by most men. Read the literature of the day. That was just the culture. You go on a tour, and you see where the men were, the athletic areas and public spas, and right next door were where the illicit sexual activities were, constantly available and constantly appropriated. The opportunities were endless.

Genuine emotional, sexual, marital love is emotional intimacy of the highest degree, and for most men and women of the first century, that glue was absent in their marriage. Marriage, as God designed it in the garden of Eden, was designed to make a man "cleave" to his wife, which literally meant "to be glued together." To find this bond that could not be broken, that was tightly knit, fitted together.

Salvation stopped much of the immorality, but getting saved did not automatically make husbands and wives instantly close or intimate or life-sharing friends or lovers. Just as modern premarital moral laxity has scarred many young couples into a troubled, often superficial marital relationship, so were most of the marriages of the New Testament Church.

Physical love without romance is soon empty and meaningless, and as Solomon, who had a lot of experience, said, it becomes like gravel in the mouth. So what was Paul's Spirit-prompted answer to that problem? What was God's way to protect those distant, detached, constantly tempted husbands who were daily buffeted with the overpowering allurements of a flagrantly immoral society? What did Paul say was the device to help those men out there?

Christ led Paul to deploy a legion of older-in-the-faith women who would become close and trusted friends of those young wives, and to train them how to become the best and most intimate friends to their husbands. Paul knew that to protect those newly believing husbands and fathers from the tidal wave of temptations, they must have a vibrant, satisfying emotional and physical relationship with their wife.

Husbands who are drawn to think about and want to see their wife throughout the day while they're away from home are protected from the attractions and distractions that a wicked world produces. A best friend is someone you think about, someone you go toward, who you're drawn to, who you pursue. So Paul told Titus to fill the Church with wives learning to be their husbands' best friends. And loving, caring, romantic wives who love their husbands in this biblical way come through the biblical example of older, grace-energized women who said to them, "If God can change me, God can change you."

If you've ever wondered why some of the most amazing men have left some of the most amazing wives for some un-amazing person at work, it's because of the one thing that is missing in the otherwise amazing marriage, and it's the one thing that person at work gives him. She admires him. She tells him he is the best salesman or the best manager or the best mechanic or whatever. She looks up to him, she admires him, she respects him, and she tells him so. But to the wife, he's just the husband. And men gravitate to where admiration and respect flow. Sometimes it's with another woman, or sometimes it's out with the guys. And the wife asks why he'd rather sit out in the woods in the rain and the cold with his feet in ice water than to be with her. He'll still do his responsibilities, but his heart goes where he feels respect and love and admiration and acceptance.

Men deeply need the emotional friendship of an accepting, caring, seeking, admiring, and pursuing woman in their lives. If you doubt that, ask yourself why so many men leave their wives for the woman who chased them at work. Yes, it's a sin to commit adultery, but much adultery starts in men seeking the admiration and longing for the respect, and finding the friendship and closeness his wife is showing to her girlfriends, mother, sisters, and children, but rarely to him. God commands wives to love their husband with a love he can feel. And love-filled, respect-reflecting wives find themselves becoming their husband's best friend, exactly as God designed them to be.

Best Friend in All the World

Have you ever met a man who's still alone even though he's married? He's just looking for things to fill his life, looking for places to go. He never wants to go home. I remember when I was single, I'd work alongside married men and I'd be ready to go, and they'd ask where I was going. So I'd tell them, and they'd say, "Can I go with you?" And I'd ask, "Aren't you married? Don't you want to go home?" They're alone while they're married. That's not a new problem. That's an old problem.

Titus faced the same problem on Crete, a whole group of married men who were alone even though they were married. Their lives were unshared. Their initiatives were not responded to. Their leadership was not fully followed. Their marriages and homes were, as a result, far from God's plan. And so the solution was found in God's call for, not only Spirit-prompted *agape* love, which was to be present in the life of every believer, but in the close, relational *phileo* love of a best friend.

You will start a whole new chapter of your marriage and open an entirely new dimension to your relationship when you realize that God Himself designed your husband or wife just for you. All the differences you have in perspective, in taste, in personality, in mood, and in ability are placed there by God for His glory and your good. And however you came to be married, it is God's desire for you to learn and cultivate and practice and make it your aim to be a Titus 2 woman who loves her husband.

Loving Your Own Man

Young women, just saved out of paganism, needed to get accustomed to a whole new set of priorities and privileges. And those with unsaved husbands would need special encouragement. So they learned and were trained in how to respect and admire and encourage their own husband. They learned how to build him up, how to surprise him with their affection. They learned how to cultivate a lifelong growing and deepening friendship. But what are some practical steps the Titus 2 woman would teach?

When we first moved to California in the early eighties, a godly older woman in that church invited my wife over to her house for tea, and this is what she shared with her. Decide to make your husband your number one most important human relationship in life. Begin to seek your husband's friendship and love. Examine your lifestyle and schedule to see if you are intentionally spoiling your husband rotten.

Check your schedule, your weekly schedule, to see if you are intentionally pursuing your husband's love, seeking his interests, and gaining his attention. Any man will notice the interest shined on him by an adoring woman. And may he find that from you.

This is a high calling from God, to be your husband's best friend, because if you're examining your schedule, you'll have to take something out to put him in. You have to alter your life. And so the godly woman who mentored my wife gave her several practical ways to maintain this high calling. It was a list of nine simple things to do every day, and I found the handwritten notes she took, and it was all worn out, so I typed them out and put it back. These truths worked. And I hope they help you.

- **Pray for your husband daily.** If you love someone, you don't have to be reminded to pray for them daily. I remember early in our marriage, my wife kept asking me, every morning, all the things I'd be doing that day so that she could pray for me all throughout the day. And so I'd try to think of things, and then when I got home, she'd ask me about all those things. And I was shocked she'd remembered them, but she'd been praying for them all day long. And I thought, wow. I don't pray for her all day long. I need to do that.

- **Plan for him daily.** This would be things like special acts of kindness, special dinners, special times alone, special meals alone, early bedtime for the children, going to bed at the same time. Plan for him, daily things. Do those seem like little things? It's big. When your best friend is planning special things for you, you'll never forget that.

- **Prepare for him daily.** Prepare your heart by being clothed with God's love. Prepare your house. Prepare your appearance. Prepare your greeting when he gets home. Set the table. Clear out all the visitors. Stay off the phone. Pray about his arrival. I remember when I used to come home, it actually appeared that my wife was waiting for me. And when the kids got older, there was this window where I parked the car, and I'd see a little head in the window when I got home. Then two years later, two little heads, then three, then four. And I remember asking my wife, why are the kids always looking out the window? And she said, because we prepare for you coming home. This isn't to literally stick all your kids in the window for your husband when he gets home. It's find ways to prepare for him. It's that best friend who lights up when they see you. Does that characterize your marriage?

- **Please him daily.** Think about how you can please your husband, whether it's in how you dress, or in putting on perfume just before he gets home, be sure you are intentionally doing things to please your husband. Your number one human relationship is your husband, so be sure that you are preparing for him, whether anyone else sees you all day or not. You want to love your husband with a love he can feel? Think about what pleases him.

- **Protect your time with him.** This is a big challenge for husbands and wives, especially in our busy culture, with so many distractions that are pulling us in multiple directions, and especially if you have children that seem to demand so much of your time, but more than your hobbies or career or children or anything else, protect the time you spend with your husband. Be sure to schedule regular date nights, get a babysitter, set aside a few minutes every morning just to be together before he goes to work. Whatever form it takes, do not let anything crowd out your time with the person God escorted you to and made for you.

- **Physically love him.** Let him know that you are available. God commands us in Proverbs to be intoxicated with the love of our partner.[34] If you are married and not intoxicated by the love of your partner, you are missing the best marriage possible.

- **Positively respond to him.** I remember when I first shared an idea with my wife about having a dinner for the deacons. She could have told me all the problems there would be, but instead, she responded positively to me. She encouraged me. She said, "That's a great idea. Let's invite the wives," and then she took my idea and helped me make it a reality. She was my helper, the one who came alongside and made my ministry flourish. She got the tables set up and decorated and she made my idea a success. This is what it means in Proverbs 31 when it says her husband is known at the city gates. He is successful and is known at the gates because his wife wants to see him succeed.

---

34 Proverbs 5:18–19

- **Praise him.** Again, this goes back to the respect-reflecting aspect of this *phileo* love that wives are supposed to have. If you respect your husband in your heart, but you never tell him you're proud of him, you never praise him, you never encourage him, you never point out what he's doing that you admire, then he is not being loved with a love he can feel. Women tend to gossip about their husbands when they get together, but a godly Titus 2 wife doesn't do that. In fact, she doesn't say anything negative about him, not to her mother, not to her girlfriends, not in front of her children. She makes it a point to praise her husband instead.
- **Pray without ceasing.** This one is so important it's in there twice. Never stop praying for your husband. And never stop letting him know you're praying for him. This is one of the most important, if not the most important ministry you can have for your husband.

In designing marriage the way He did in Genesis 2, God was declaring a vital truth: that if you choose to live your life contrary to His design, it will not work. If you try to live and go through life in marriage in a way other than what it was designed to be, it becomes what Proverbs calls a constant dripping, like lying in a tent in the rain with a leak in it. Few things are as miserable as a marriage that God compares to Chinese water torture, and it's because the marriage is not operating on the original settings that God designed.

But if you choose, today, to begin cultivating the kind of marriage and the kind of love that God says has the power to change the world, then you will begin to find in your marriage what Adam found in his that made him say, "This is it! The thing I searched the whole world for!" The close, intimate, best-friendship-in-all-the-world, where both you and your spouse find absolute contentment and satisfaction in being each other's missing piece. And the world will see it, and they will want what you have. The rewards are worth the investment.

God has called godly women to be a beacon of Christ's love, to reflect, in the midst of an empty and hopeless world, that true marital love is possible. And not just possible. You can have it for a lifetime.

Father, I thank You that You designed a way to impact a pagan culture, because our culture is getting more pagan all the time. Your power is the same, Your desires haven't changed, and we have the same challenges. And I pray that we would become reflectors of Your Word in our daily lives. I thank You that Your Word is true, powerful, and practical. It changed the Roman Empire, it changed the island of Crete, and it changed the individual lives in those churches as those older women trained the younger women. Give us the faith to believe You, to accept the power You're giving us to change our lives, our marriages, and our families. And we pray this in the name of Jesus, and for His glory. Amen.

Respond to Truth

How does your marriage compare to the factory settings? If God were to reset you back to His original plan, what parts of your life would He have to change?

How does *agape* love differ from the *phileo* love Titus 2 talks about? What kind of love do you have for your husband?

How does God call a believing wife to love her husband if he's an unbe-liever (1 Peter 3:1–6)?

If someone asked your husband if you love him, what would he say? What if they asked how he knows you love him? Would he be able to point to your choices as proof that you put him first?

Who is your number one human relationship? What practical choices can you make today to make it your husband?

Grace-Energized Mothers | 8

Titus 2:4 contains the first two priorities for older women to teach to younger women. The first is that they love their husbands. But the second, "to love their children," seems almost too obvious. Of course mothers are to love their children, and if a mother doesn't love her children, we as a society feel outrage. But in the Roman society, true biblical love was so far removed from everyday life that mothers needed to be taught how to love their children with a love they could feel.

NURTURING LOVE IN A LOVELESS WORLD

The culture of Rome was driven by mighty armies. When people thought of Rome, they thought of those fearless Legionnaires who would march into the face of death. They were not weak, wimpy, sentimental men. They were tough. It was also a culture framed by overpowering architecture. Some of the grandest and most impossible engineering projects, aqueducts that defied gravity and brought water to every home, still exist to this day. And of course the emperors were known for their incredible power, for holding life and death in their hands. That's the culture of Rome. Strength and toughness were elevated, and love wasn't spoken of.

In the Roman Empire, they practiced *pater potestes*, which was the all-encompassing power of the father. When a baby was born and they got it all cleaned up and wrapped up, they'd bring and place the baby in front of the father, and he could choose to keep the baby in the family or not. And if not, they'd put the baby out with the garbage. That's where a lot of prostitutes and gladiators came from, those discarded babies who were picked up and raised by people who would roam around like people do today after a garage sale to see what gets left out on the curb.

In a culture such as this, those who were loving and sensitive and caring were viewed as being weak. In the Roman Empire, love, as expressed the way the Bible describes it, was considered a weakness to be dealt with and gotten rid of. Only the tough could endure all the hardness of the day in which Paul lived, so the introduction of love as the top quality that wives and mothers were to possess must have been shocking to those early believers. This went counter to their whole culture, their whole society. Because love was never seen in everyday life, this gentle, sensitive, nurturing love was to be a powerful witness in a very dark culture.

Maybe you grew up in an environment like Rome, in an environment of conflict and hatred. Others have known and felt the warmth of a loving parent's embrace and known the encouragement of their words of affirmation and loving investment. For every person who heard this letter read, it called for a lifestyle change, for social non-conformity. It offended their peers who were not living this way. But if you want to please God, then God calls you to shape your family through love.

So how did these God-seeking younger women, who'd never seen this modeled, who'd never seen this done, learn how to be wives and mothers characterized by love? Through the godly mentoring relationship of older women of grace in Christ's Church. And what did those older women say? What lessons did they teach? Well, let me just suggest a few. If you were following a Titus 2 older woman into a Cretan home in the first century, these are the things an older mother might say to a younger mother who just came to Christ, who was overwhelmed.

1. She would explain that negative feelings in certain circumstances toward your own children are normal, even for a mature believer.

Many of us look at the early church members like superheroes. They were the ones who would fly in and solve all the problems. They had something different from what we have, something more, because they saw the resurrection or because they knew the Apostle Paul or whatever. The very fact that Paul commanded them to love their children tells us that the first century saints found this unnatural and difficult.

Almost all mothers love their children, but it's an equally true fact that it often gets very hard to take care of children, and so while they may have that sacrificial love for their children, doing the duty, many mothers come to a place where they no longer feel love toward their children.

Imagine how that would liberate that young mother. To sometimes feel negatively toward your children is normal. Why? Because they're childish. Because they do things that are wrong. Because they're sinners, and you're a sinner. Now, these feelings are not to be sustained, they're not to be allowed, they're not to be perpetuated and allowed to grow and fester, but they are normal.

2. She would explain that God's plan for His Church was for younger women to need the mentoring help of older women.

God's plan for tired and burned out and depressed mothers to get relief is from the faithful army of Titus 2 grace-energized older women who are role models. God designed it. It's right here in Titus 2. The absence of it is abnormal. Women were not to primarily learn how to parent from the multitude of Christian authors. Those are supplements, but we're not supposed to live on vitamins. We're supposed to live on food. And the food a young mother is to live on is that coming-alongside nurturing, mentoring help of a godly older woman who can model for her what being a loving mother looks like.

3. She would show her how families are vulnerable to the cultural trends that slowly seep in.

As a godly priority, loving your children seems almost too obvious to mention, but there were forces at work in the family back then, and today, that work to undermine even this most basic principle of loving your children. Women are being told that their interest and desires come first, that they have to do what makes them happy before they can be good wives and mothers, but while women should be encouraged to use their gifts and abilities, each Christian woman should be taught to align her priorities with God's priorities, not the world's wisdom. She must love her husband. She must love her children. Love brings sacrifices. And God will honor those who value what He values.

And so, those godly older women could show the younger women how centuries of the Cretan lifestyle had seeped into their godly homes. How they were used to lying, how they were used to being lazy, how they were used to being undisciplined, but that is not how we're to be in Christ.

These cultural trends can devastate family life. You want to know one for us? For the twenty-first century? Because of all the athletic events and all the extracurricular activities, families no longer gather as a unit. They basically eat walking around, and with the constant intrusion of the telephone and the constant sound of the television in the background and the constant demands of society, the family is fragmented, and there is rarely a Deuteronomy 6 model. Remember Deuteronomy 6? You speak the Word of God to your kids as you walk together and as you have bedtime together and as you eat together. Today, there's this absence of a word-filled family because of the cultural trends that seep in. That's something a godly older woman would point out and warn against.

4. She would show her the biblical perspective of motherhood.

Do you know how God sees motherhood? That children are a gift from the Lord, and that a woman is saved from having an inferior place to a man, by completely fulfilling God's calling to raise her children. And there are mothers who have physical children, and mothers who have spiritual children. And both are considered a high calling from God.

Every woman is to be the thermostat for the home, setting a tone of warmth and love. This love is phileo love. Philoteknos, "children-lovers." And it means to have affection for. It is not just expressed, it is intentionally directed toward someone that they may feel it. It is demonstrated by time and tenderness and by the eyes and by the touch and by the desired closeness. And it is a grace-energized mother's special ministry in Christ's church. Paul is saying that mothers are to not just serve their children, but to have the deep emotional friendship, the love of accompanying and being near them and of enjoying them. And whether you're a wife and a mother, or a father, or a young person, or a not so young person, the same spirit of God, the same grace from God, wants the same response from all of us.

Homemaking and child-rearing are not second-place ministries. They are among the highest priorities in Christ's church, and they should be the highest priorities of a godly woman of grace. God has such a high opinion of wives and mothers that he placed learning to love one's husband and love one's children as the top two things a younger woman should be taught.

5. She would assure that young mother that she doesn't have any unique challenges.

The Word of God is supra-cultural. It's timeless. It meets every need in every culture. The Greek culture taught that a woman was nothing more than a producer of children and wasn't to leave the home; the Roman culture pressed women into leaving the home and being a career woman, and both pressures are still present today.

Your issues are not new. Every challenge, no matter how big and no matter how small, is to be met and dealt with God's way, no matter what the culture says. This is what the godly older women of the church would teach and model, and this is what would shine as a light to a very dark culture, two thousand years ago, and still today.

NURTURING LOVE: DISCIPLING LIKE THE APOSTLE PAUL

Do you know how Paul described his discipleship method? He described himself as a nursing mother and a loving father. I bet you've never gone to a discipleship class like that! But the way that Paul loved his children in the faith is a model for all godly mothers who want to love their children with a love they can feel.

Timothy, that mighty pastor of probably the largest church of the New Testament, the church at Ephesus, with this thriving congregation, was a very needy man. If you know anything about Timothy, you know he was weak in constitution, often infirm and sick. People looked down on him. He cried a lot. We never hear about his dad, only about his mother and grandmother.

Paul loved Timothy, his son in the faith, and so as our model, we ask how Paul showed Timothy love that he could feel. How was that love expressed? It's one of the most beautiful testimonies to the power of encouragement and affirmation in the New Testament.

Paul called Timothy "a true son," said he was an "example to the flock," and that he had a gift.[35] He reminded him of his great spiritual heritage and was careful not to belittle him for his weaknesses or his frequent tears.[36] Rather, he told Timothy he had a treasure entrusted to him and that God was going to use him.[37]

Nurturing love attaches a high value to the person you love. We should always remember that hugs aren't enough. Tell your children how you feel about them. Those that are left to fill in the blanks are often left feeling worthless and insecure. At best, only confusion can come from silence. Far too many of us are really not that encouraging. It's not that we have a critical spirit. It's just that we don't say anything. Our loved ones are not mind-readers. We can do better than just expecting them to know they're loved and admired and sought out by us. Instead of making them guess, they need to hear it.

Grace-energized mothers tell their children the qualities they admire in them. One of the best ways to do this is to liken them to something precious, such as calling your daughter a pearl or a precious jewel. With your husband, this can be communicated by calling him a wonderful dad, husband, and friend, a faithful leader and provider, diligent, hard-working, thoughtful, etc. For a husband to attach high value to his wife, this comes in the form of telling her he thought about her all day long, that he can't wait to see her, that he knows how hard she works all day and can't wait to

---

35   1 Timothy 1:2, 4:12, 4:14
36   2 Timothy 3:15; 1 Timothy 5:23; 2 Timothy 1:4
37   1 Timothy 6:20; 2 Timothy 4:8

get home to help her, that there are so many things he wants to talk over with her, that he'd rather spend time with her, walking and talking, than to be out with the guys.

The absence of loving approval can lead to a lot of pain, whereas those who are loved can face their daily challenges in the world they live in with strength and confidence that someone loves them. Make an effort to catch them doing something good, something right, something thoughtful, something considerate, something well-done, and point it out, and say, "that was wonderful." That was Paul's model with Timothy and it is the kind of nurturing love that every mother should employ.

Nurturing love also envisions a bright future for the loved one. How many of you remember your parents ever looking you straight in the eye, putting their hands on your shoulder, and saying, "I love you. You are the most wonderful child. I am so grateful God gave you to me. I believe God made you for a purpose." If they did that, you remember it. If they didn't, you remember it.

Paul envisioned a bright future for Timothy. There was a crown awaiting him as he ran the race set before him. Paul told Timothy the Lord was going to reward him. "Timothy, I'm going on ahead, but on that day, God is going to give me a crown, but not just to me. To you too." He painted for Timothy a bright future if he'd just keep following the Lord, so we also should express what God can do with our children if they follow Him in their lives.

Grace-energized mothers explain to their children how they can become the greatest servant of the Lord in whatever field God has gifted them. Explain why you think their gifts and character traits will be useful throughout their lives. Avoid the overuse of negative admonitions. The New Testament uses the word "bless" forty-four times, and it means to audibly praise your loved one, to celebrate your loved one, asking God to bless the one you love, to prosper them, to make them happy, or to rain down upon them God's favor. Use biblical affirmations to inspire confident dependence on God.

I remember being at the hospital as my dad was dying. My dad had made it a point, once a week from the time I graduated from college, to call me, wherever I was. And I wish I had tape recordings of it, it was so wonderful. He'd tell me he was praying for me, and he wanted to know what I was doing that week so he could pray, and he always said, "I want you to know that God made you for special purposes, and He's got a plan, and He's bringing it to pass." Do you know he did that for thirty years? And when he was lying there with all those tubes in him and all the IVs, and he was dying, he reached up and pulled off that oxygen mask so that with his last breath he could say, "I love you. I've prayed for you all your life. Keep serving the Lord." And he put the mask back on and died about three minutes later.

I hope you never forget the power you have as parents of love. And I hope that your children have heard you say with all your heart that you love them. Make sure that they hear that you love them.

The Power of Words

We need to consider that many children are hurt because they sense that their parents don't even like them. When a struggling student watches their mother gloat about their brother or sister's good grades, they immediately feel less because of the comparison. If a boy doesn't do well in some athletic event and looks up and immediately sees his father's look of disappointment because the father was the great athlete, he does not feel love.

Many husbands feel that their wives admire other men more than them, because their wives say, "so and so's husband does this and that with his children and his wife," and immediately, those husbands don't feel the love and admiration of their wife. They feel that she thinks more highly of someone else because they're compared. Many wives feel their husbands think other women are better at caring for their families than they are for the same reason. And in the same way, many children do not feel the love of their parents when they are compared to someone else.

Another way that children can be hurt by our words is when we use humor in a way that puts them down. Not to be mean, but because it's funny. But if the person isn't laughing, it's not a joke. It's harmful to them. Our words have power, and they can either communicate a nurturing love that our children can feel, or they communicate something very different.

That's why the Apostle Paul didn't just speak whatever came to mind. He prepared special words for those he loved, and that is seen in this passage of 1 Thessalonians:

"We speak, not as pleasing men, but God who tests our hearts. We were gentle among you, just as a nursing mother cherishes her own children. You know how we exhorted, and comforted, and charged every one of you, as a father does his own children. When you received the word of God which you heard from us, you welcomed it not as the word of men, but as it is in truth, the word of God, which also effectively works in you who believe. Therefore we wanted to come to you—even I, Paul, time and again—but Satan hindered us. For what is our hope, or joy, or crown of rejoicing? Is it not even you in the presence of our Lord Jesus Christ at His coming? For you are our glory and joy."[38]

This is God describing a nurturing heart. Look at how Paul speaks to this congregation. His example shows us the power our words can have when we take the time to prepare special words for our children out of nurturing love. But what is the content of his speech?

Nurturing love communicates the truth of God that people need to hear. If you're feeding a child, you don't just give him gummy bears. You make sure he gets the protein and the fiber and the vegetables. Paul is saying he didn't just speak what made the Thessalonians happy. Pleasing God is always in the backdrop. Paul was gripped by, and his nurturing love was formed by, what pleased God, and telling them what they needed to do to please God. He communicates the truth of God. There's a content to nurturing love.

The next one, verse 7, says, "We were gentle among you just as a nursing mother cherishes her own children." Nurturing love is tenderly directed toward an individual's needs. You don't use a serving spoon filled with castor oil and jam it in a child's mouth. It's okay to get grape and bubblegum flavor, and each child needs God's truth gently provided to them individually. There's something very tender about nurturing love that tailors itself to a child's individual needs.

By the way, you've heard of Saint Augustine? When he preached on this passage, he said this Greek word "gentle among you," is what you see

---

38   1 Thessalonians 2:4, 7, 11, 13, 18–20

when a parent is talking in baby talk to their child. You've seen it, this big, huge, six-foot-four guy with this tiny thing in his arms and talking to him in a way he'd never speak in public. That's how Paul nurtured and loved.

The next one has three levels of nurturing love that are described in one verse. "We exhorted, and comforted, and charged every one of you." Nurturing love needs to be clearly communicated in many ways, on many levels. The exhortation is the first level. The comfort is the second kind. And the charging is the third kind. Whether it's an emphatic, "come on," or a gentle pleading, "come on," or a matter-of-fact, calling someone to their senses "come on," love needs to be communicated on many levels. In fact, one of the words used here, *paramutheo*, means to "whisper in the ear."

Years ago, we lived in this house that was built before central heating, and it had no hallways, and you'd have to walk through every room to get to the other room, so when I'd have a five-thirty discipleship meeting and a six-thirty leadership meeting, I'd sneak out of the house without turning on the lights so I wouldn't wake anybody up.

One day I went to my five-thirty discipleship meeting and met with a whole group of men, and then sat with a whole other group of men for the leadership meeting at six-thirty, then I went for a cup of coffee at seven-thirty so I'd be at the office by eight, and Channel 3 news was there. And because I was the pastor at Quidnessett Church, which was a very large New England church, they said, "and now we have the pastor of Quidnessett Church," and they had that great big camera right on my face. And I was standing there with my donut and my coffee and I answered their question about some issue, then I got to the office and my sweet, seventy-eight-year-old secretary looked right at me and said, "did you know you have your sweater on backwards?"

I had slipped it on backward, quietly, in the dark, and there I was on the evening news with my sweater on backward, and you know what? Everyone at that breakfast saw that. Everyone on the leadership team saw that. But no one would *paramutheo* me. No one would come alongside and whisper to me what I needed to hear. Nurturing love doesn't do that. It comes alongside and whispers in the ear what the person needs to hear on every level, whether exhortation, or comfort, or a direct charge.

The next element is found in verse 13, where Paul says, "When you received the word of God which you heard from us, you welcomed it, not as the word of men, but as it is in truth, the word of God." Nurturing love involves encouraging individuals, not to listen to us, but to invite them to listen to the Word of God.

Remember Philip and the Ethiopian eunuch? Philip met that Ethiopian eunuch where he was in his chariot, explained the word of God to him and kept explaining it and kept helping him until he got that Ethiopian's hand connected to the Lord's. That's what parenting is all about. We hold our children's hands, but we're progressively lifting that hand up and introducing them until we get our children to hold the Lord's hand.

Our children listen to us because they see us and trust us and know us, and they feel our love, but what we keep bringing them back to is God's Word so that they see it's not us directing them to live that way, that it's not us exhorting them to forsake that sin or that wasteful part of their life. It's God. Nurturing love is all about getting them to respond to the Word of God, and that's what Paul was so gifted at.

Look at verse 18. Nurturing love persists even when facing great hardships and difficulties because it's prompted by God. In verse 18, Paul talks about Satan putting up roadblocks. This is a Roman legion word, when the mighty army would be marching along and someone would put a roadblock in their path to stop the progress of the Roman Legionnaires in their tracks. And that's what Satan was doing, preventing Paul from going to see the Thessalonians, but Paul persevered, because that's what nurturing love does.

If you're close enough that you're nurturing someone and you're walking close enough that you're getting them to hold the Lord's hand, all of a sudden it hurts. They're going to have to start forsaking things. They have to start mortifying things and rooting them out. Remember Samuel in the Old Testament? Saul neglected to kill King Agag when he defeated his armies, and Samuel reached over and pulled the sword out of somebody's scabbard, and he hacked Agag to pieces. Do you know what that's a picture of? You don't have mercy on the flesh, on God's enemy. You don't tolerate sin. And this can get hard. But nurturing love persists.

The last one is found in verses 19–20. "For what is our hope, or joy, or crown of rejoicing? Is it not even you in the presence of our Lord Jesus Christ at His coming? For you are our glory and joy." Nurturing love produces endless rewards in heaven, because investment in people is the only thing we can take with us to heaven. You can't take your boat, your collection, your restored car, your intricately built home or manicured garden. You can only take people. "What is our hope, or joy, or crown of rejoicing?" What do we live for? What lasts forever? People. He's taking these people with him and they are his crown in heaven because he made a deep and impactful and abiding investment in people.

Nurturing love places a high value on the person we love; it envisions a bright future for that loved one; it prepares special words for them by communicating the truth of God's Word that people need to hear (verse 4), tenderly tailored and directed to individual needs (verse 7), clearly communicating at every level and in many ways (verse 11), encouraging individuals to listen and respond to God through His word (verse 13), persisting even under adversity (verse 18), and producing an endless reward (verse 19–20). The early church was a haven of nurturing love because people were taught how to love this way. And our homes too can be a haven of such love when we follow the biblical example written down for us in God's Word.

The Greatest Quality for a Woman of Grace

In Titus 2, there is one word that sums up what a woman energized by God's grace, what a wife energized by God's grace, and what a mother who is empowered by the Spirit of God who is energized by God's grace is like, and that word is "love."

God is love. The greatest of all Christian virtues is love. And love that is energized by God's grace lasts forever. What can be the most powerful aspect of a wife and mother's life on earth obeying God's calling? What can matter most for eternity in the life of a wife and the life of a mother? What does God say will last forever from the endless and mostly unseen hours of work that being a wife and mother entail? Love. All the deeds that are offered in obedience to the Lord that are produced by grace-energized love last forever. Every moment of them.

Imagine a first-century woman, hearing this message for the first time, and she is married to a boorish, unbelieving man who lives like a Roman man lives, and she's trapped in that house, and she sees all the exciting comings and goings from the church to the furthest reaches of the empire and the incredible ministries going on, and she hears, for the first time, that what she does in that house, for that man, and for his children, if it is done in love, earns rewards in heaven the same as Barnabas earned going out with Paul on his missionary journeys.

Jesus says that you can't even give away a cup of cold water in His name without getting eternal rewards for it. Those deeds, those acts, those desires that are expressions of our God who is love—you will never lose any of those. And for a first century woman, trapped in her home, this was a liberating thought. That if she would connect her marriage, her parenting, her housework to the love of God, then everything she did in that context would last forever, and she would have God's favor and approval and eternal rewards.

Our gifts and our ministries will all one day cease to exist.[39] They will all cease to have purpose and meaning. But showing love in the context of Titus 2 to our children, practicing that love and living that love now are of utmost importance, more important than having any other virtue or gift, because love is the link God gives us with His eternal self.[40]

Love is eternal, love is supreme, and love is most like God, for God is love. First John 4:8 says "God is love." It's who He is. And when we express His love, we are most connected to Him. Jesus says that of all the Christian virtues that are meant to be reflections of His character, love is the one that the world will see and will recognize immediately as being from God. "By this all will know that you are My disciples, if you have love."[41]

First Peter 4:8 says love covers a multitude of sins. It throws a blanket over, it covers up an awful pile of sins. Love gives family life the flavor of God. But if love covers a multitude of sins, then when love is neglected, when love is absent, it causes a multitude of sins in the home, in the marriage, in the family.

Titus 2 tells us the reason that grace-energized women are to be characterized by love. It's because, verse 5, if you are not known for these things,

---

39 1 Corinthians 13:8–13
40 Paraphrased from a sermon of John MacArthur's
41 John 13:35

for love of your husbands and love of your children, if you do not love, then the word of God is blasphemed. Love is the first thing younger women are to learn, and they are to be taught by the godly example of women who are already known for their love that is like God.

> *Lord, teach us to love our children, and to love them with a love that can be felt. Whether it is a first-time mother or a mother of many, we all need Your love to transform our love for our children. And I pray for every young mother out there, that she will find an older woman in the faith who knows what it is to be exhausted and knows what it is to be overwhelmed and who knows how to nurture her children and can show that young woman how to be a children-lover. And for any who have no children of their own, that they would be the spiritual mothers of many children and would raise up a generation of godly young men and women for You. In Your name we pray, amen.*

Respond to Truth

How did Jesus model *phileo* love for His disciples (Mark 1:31, 1:41, 5:41, 7:33, 9:27, 9:36, 10:13, 10:16)?

As a practical love gift to your children, do you have:

A heart that prays for your children? A heart that trusts in the Lord? (See Isaiah 26:6.)

A heart that rejoices and is filled with happiness (Psalm 113:9)? That plays and is full of fun? That celebrates your children's special days (Matthew 5:41)?

A heart that is focused and seeks the things that matter (Matthew 6:24, 33)?

A heart that is present and attentive (Psalm 119:10)? That prefers your family first (Titus 2:4)? That serves and meets their needs with love?

A heart that gives like Christ (Mark 10:45)? That is generous (2 Corinthians 9:6)? Expecting nothing back (Luke 6:35)?

9 | Grace-Energized Minds

THE BATTLEFIELD OF THE MIND

The God who Loves Absolutes

Jesus' ministry was characterized by absolutes. He loved to bring people to the place where they realized they only had two choices in front of them. They had to choose between life and death, or between heaven and hell, or between the broad way and the narrow way, or between light and darkness, having the Son or not having the Son. Jesus always reduced it to two choices. There wasn't anything in between.

That concept, those absolutes, that choice that needs to be made, carries on into His Church. And we are presented consistently by Paul, by Peter, by James, with a choice. Either God's way, or our own way. There is no middle ground. As a Christian, you can't be half and half. Jesus said you can't serve two masters. You can't serve God and something else. You have to go entirely one way.

The third quality of a godly younger woman, after loving her husband and loving her children, is to be "discreet," Titus 2:5. And in this one word, that God chose and the Apostle Paul, under the inspiration of the Holy Spirit, wrote down for us brings us to that point, of making a choice.

"Discreet" is that word *sophron*, that every person in the Church, whether older or younger, man or woman, is supposed to have. And the choice God is calling us to make is who gets control of our mind.

The One Who Gets the Mind

God wants your mind under His control. More than anything, He wants to saturate, influence, fill, direct, dominate, and control our minds. The spiritual realm is in our mind. Our bodies, our flesh, our emotions, everything else influences that, but the spiritual meeting place between us and God is in our mind. He meets with us in our minds. That's where we pray and communicate with Him, where His Word ministers to our spirits as He energizes us by His grace. It's all in the mind, which is why the mind is so important.

If God has your mind, He has your body. If God has your mind, He has your emotions. If God has your mind, He has your appetites. If God has your mind, He has your time. If God has your mind, He has your money.

The battle is for our mind. The one who gets the mind gets it all. That's why, from the beginning, Satan has been trying to steal the minds of God's children. And it hasn't changed. In first century Crete, there were so many competing voices for the minds of the believers. That's why in verse 5, Paul tells Titus that God wants our minds.

Our mind is the key to knowing God, and only a mind stayed on the Lord, as Isaiah 26 says, can have perfect peace. Only a mind devoted to the Lord follows God's plan and purpose for our lives. God has a plan for our mind, and that is to be given to the pursuit of pleasing Him. A mind devoted to Christ is the road to God's plan for our life that He unfolds one step at a time as we yield in obedience to Him. God wants our mind. He wants it given to the pursuit of His rule, His Word, and the glory of Christ. And the grace-energized life of Titus 2 is a roadmap for how to focus our minds on what glorifies and magnifies the Lord. It's the goal, the purpose, the reason for our existence: to glorify Him.

God wants us to have a God-controlled mind. And either we choose to have a word-filled, God-controlled, Spirit-led mind and the stability and clarity and power that comes with that, or we give in to what the world offers us, a media-saturated mind, driven by whatever is currently pushing on our emotions or our heart. All that is contained in that one little word, *sophron*.

This word is so huge that it's virtually untranslatable by any one English word. It's translated "discreet" in the NKJV, and in other translations, "of sound mind," "prudent," "self-controlled," "sensible," "chaste," or "having complete control over sensual desires."

The Greeks get *sophron* from two Greek words that meant to keep one's mind safe and sound. It was a guarded mind, a mind that was protected. In Titus 2:5, this word describes a woman with a mind surrendered to God's control. That's what the older women were to encourage the younger women toward having, a mind that is regularly and consistently surrendered to God.

This is not automatic. Either you consciously surrender your mind to God's control, or your mind will slowly become desensitized and squeezed and conformed to the world around you. Either you give your mind to God, surrender to God's gracious power, learning to govern every instinct and passion until each has its proper place and no more, or you're not doing that. So if God doesn't have control of your mind, who does?

SATAN'S PLAN TO NEUTRALIZE YOUR MIND

Satan has caught many believers off guard. While they carefully avoid many doctrinal dangers, perhaps the most powerful mind-robber has been overlooked. Satan has been neutralizing the power of so many godly minds little by little, day by day, by the onslaught of those things that keep us from being focused on God.

Shock Threshold

So what would keep an individual from being *sophron*, serious about spiritual things? What would cause us to not live a disciplined life, not be self-controlled, to encourage us to be addicted to something, to seek excesses? What would start controlling our choices if it wasn't God?

It is Satan's constant desire to keep us from the mind of God. Our mind is the meeting place where the world, the flesh, and the devil are in constant conflict against the Spirit of God and His Word, and there is this constant battle in our mind.

So how does Satan get us? How does he constantly bombard our mind? For a moment, just think about the world you live in. First of all, your godly mind can get neutralized by modern media—music, videos, games, the Internet, going to the movies, watching TV, reading magazines and newspapers. Media has reset the shock threshold.

In the past, if we saw blood, killing, or tragedy on the evening news, it would disturb us for weeks. I remember the Kent State tragedy in the seventies where they shot that student and you saw on the news the blood running down and it was just awful. The whole nation got sick. Now? Blood, killing, and tragedies are the rule of the newsroom. If it bleeds, it leads.

Movies are worse. Since the seventies, there have been succeeding waves of movies that relied on more and more violence to attract the crowds, and audiences became numb to the repulsiveness of the violence, and directors had to enhance the horror to keep their attention.

Such violent fare no longer elicits anguish from society, but what's most troubling is that believers are no longer shocked by the sin they see. It is graphically portrayed in front of us but our minds become so numbed to it that it no longer shocks us.

Morality Threshold[42]

Secondly, our godly mind can be neutralized by modern media that has reset the moral acceptability threshold.

To hold its audience, the entertainment industry feels it has to parade in front of us everything God says is wrong—adultery and promiscuity, homosexuality, incest, violence, and every other kind of sadistic thing. As a result, the lowest things have become commonplace, and worse, even morally acceptable.

Just think about it. Do things that once offended you now entertain you? Have you changed enough in the last five, ten, or fifteen years that what used to offend you right away now entertains you? Are you able to enjoy the company of television shows, movies, and games that have values that are diametrically opposed to God's? Ephesians 5:12 says, "For it is shameful

---

42   Adapted and quoted from Swenson, Overload, pp. 137–160. Adapted and quoted from Al Menconi, "Our Collective Soul Is Dying" *Minnesota Christian Chronicle, 16 February 1995, p. 6.*

even to speak of those things which are done by them in secret," let alone know them, sing them, watch them. All of this goes against a godly mind.

The bar for what we will tolerate is getting lower and lower all the time, and this continues unabated. If you were to just extrapolate out ten or twenty years, it's frightening to imagine what media content will be existing in the world around us. The world is not getting better and better. It's getting darker and darker. Every barrier is being crossed. There used to be words you couldn't say in public. There used to be images you couldn't see in public. There used to be events you would never talk about in public, but the threshold is just dropping.

First, we are no longer shocked by sin. It becomes commonplace, expected. But second, we are no longer offended by it, and it becomes accepted, to watch, to provide entertainment, and what God says is offensive and wrong and a perversion of the perfect world He created becomes to us perfectly normal. We no longer see sin for what it is, an abomination to God, and our mind becomes neutralized.

Ability to See and Communicate the Things of God

Media also reduces our linguistic powers. Many people that are heavily into media don't really know how to talk and to frame their thoughts. You talk to people who are heavily influenced by media and they don't think deeply about things, so they don't speak deeply. And most people are so entertained that they don't carry on in-depth conversations, so that affects the Christian ability to impact the world. We have a diminution of our linguistic powers and so we can't communicate about God very well.

The words of Helen Lemmel's hymn are still true. "Turn your eyes upon Jesus, look full in His wonderful face and the things of earth will grow strangely dim." But the reverse is also true. The more you fill your mind with the things of the world, the more the things of God will grow strangely dim. Satan seeks to neutralize our godly mind by media that hinders our ability to see and communicate the things of God.

If you choose to be entertained by godlessness, your mind will be calloused. If you choose to be entertained by sensuality, your mind will be defiled. If you choose to be entertained by violence, you will be desensitized to the Spirit of God. If you choose to be entertained by evil, God will seem distant from you. If you choose to be entertained by worldliness, you will be discouraged. If you choose to be entertained by Satan's way of thinking, you will forfeit the blessings of having the mind of Christ.

Let's be blunt. Don't say you're committed to Christ unless you are disciplining your mind for the active pursuit of godliness. Isaiah 33:15–17 says the only way to see God is to dwell in a place where you refrain from the things that offend Him. You stop your eyes from seeing them, you stop your ears from hearing them, and then, and only then, you will see the King in His beauty.

GOD'S PLAN: HOW TO BE A WOMAN WHO IS DISCREET

There are many ways you can study the Bible. There are book studies—you study the whole book of Genesis. There are chapter studies—you study the thirteenth chapter of 1 Corinthians. There are verse studies—you look at all the implications of one verse. There are topic studies, subject studies, thematic studies. But one of the most amazing ways to study the Bible is a word study—looking at every single occurrence of a word in the Bible, and looking at exactly what God communicates through that word.

God's Word is the best commentary on His Word, and the word *sophron* is only used to describe believers. It's found in verb form, adjective form, noun form, but it's always used of believers, and however it's used, it is something that God desires from every godly woman who makes it her goal to please Him.

Word-Filled

Another time *sophron* is used in Titus 2 is in verse 2, where it says that older men are to be temperate. Same idea. Older men are to have a serious view in life, that they are to be serious about spiritual things. All the way through life, we realize that we have a short time to live for God, a short time to redeem the time, a short time to bring glory to His name, and our whole life is going to be brought and laid before Him, and He is going to burn away everything that is not pleasing to Him. That is something to be serious about.

Does that mean we never smile and can't laugh, and shouldn't be joyful about anything? No. Humor is wonderful and laughter is good medicine, but there is a sanctifying effect in the life of a believer that keeps us from being known as a clown. That's what Gene Getz says about this word, *sophron*, that it means, "to not be known as a clown."

An elder, Titus 1:8, must be "sober-minded," same word. You don't want an elder who is constantly funny and constantly keeping everyone in stitches and clowning around all the time. Whatever you think of as the serious mind of an elder is what God says He wants from you. We still have humor and joy and a merry heart, but we should be exceedingly serious about spiritual things, about God and His kingdom and His desires for us and the direction of our life and the brevity of our life and the content of our talk. From the elders, to the older women, to the younger women, and to every member of the church, we are to be serious about spiritual things, and what keeps us from that is when we allow Satan and the world and the flesh to creep in and distract us from the mind of Christ.

To be "discreet" in Titus 2:5 is to be "serious about spiritual things." To be cautious and controlled in the way you present yourself. In another part of Scripture, in Old English, it says, "in shame-faced sobriety." That doesn't mean you have to dress in black like a Puritan and have your face pulled back by a permanent bun. It means a mind that isn't given to wandering off.

Paul put it this way in 2 Corinthians 10:5: "Bringing every thought into captivity to the obedience of Christ."

How are you doing at having a growing seriousness about spiritual things? Do you spend time with the Lord until you hear His voice in the Word? If not, why not? What hinders that? Do you constantly have the television playing in the background? Do you constantly have music playing in the background? Have you thought about the content of that rumble in the background? Are you even aware of it? Have you looked carefully at what you spend time entertained with? Is that promoting seriousness about God? Or is that promoting Satan's agenda, worldliness, and distraction?

Is your godly mind troubled that videos and movies have a deleterious effect on all of us concerning meditation? When we watch media, it shortens our attention span. That's why it's a rarity having people sitting still for twenty or thirty minutes to listen to a monologue, a lecture, or sermon. People have to be held in little twenty- and thirty-second intervals by constant changes, otherwise they lose interest. The attention span is just so shortened.

That's why it's so hard to get to know God, because it takes a long time to be still, to come before Him, to get His Word in and to yield our minds and surrender to Him, then to prayerfully engage Him in His Word. That's very hard to do if you have a shortened attention span.

God-Controlled

Sophron is defined by one commentator as "a clarity of thought that leads to an orderly life." *Sophron* is that God-controlled mind that allows us to look at the world and see it clearly, not clouded over by our limited understanding and all the world throws our way, but to have sound judgment. To see things as they really are.

How well does that describe your view of the world? Is your godly mind troubled that we have a world that is defined more by media than by God's word? Does it trouble you that our world is being defined by what is anti-God? Do you have biblical parameters constantly before you, or are you constantly assaulted by the many avenues for media to come in? History is being rewritten, moral absolutes are being reconstituted, all of it is coming so fast, and it is in constant opposition to a God-controlled mind.

When God says that He wants to control our mind, what does He mean? When He uses the word *sophron,* what is it that He expects from believers? Most of us know those great verses, Romans 12:1–2, "I beseech you therefore, brethren, by the mercies of God, that you present your bodies a living sacrifice, holy, acceptable to God, which is your reasonable service. And do not be conformed to this world, but be transformed by the renewing of your mind, that you may prove what is that good and acceptable and perfect will of God."

So, what is the will of God? After we've presented our bodies as a living sacrifice, and as our minds are being renewed by the Word of God, what is the very first thing that God wants from this sacrificial, mind-renewed life? Verse 3 "To think *sophron*, soberly."

God says not to think more highly of yourself than you're supposed to think. And don't think more lowly of yourself than you're supposed to think. But think, "so as to have sound judgment," in the NASB. Not inflated, not deflated, not an overestimation or an underestimation. We are to have our view of life defined by God. To think under God's control. That's what it means to have sound judgment, to see things clearly. And this leads us to think in a Philippians 4:8 model.

Do you remember Philippians 4:8? "Whatever things are true, whatever things are noble, whatever things are just, whatever things are pure, whatever things are lovely, whatever things are of good report, if there is any virtue and if there is anything praiseworthy—meditate on these things."

A mind that is under God's control, instantly when stuff is coming in, stops and asks if that's true, if it's honest, if it's just or slanted, if it's pure, lovely, of good report. There's a Philippians 4:8 grid that controls what is allowed into the mind to be meditated on when you have a God-controlled mind.

So how do we do that? Well, God uses the same word in 2 Timothy 1:7. "For God has not given us a spirit of fear, but of power and of love and of a sound mind." So what does a sound mind, a *sophron* mind, a God-controlled mind do when we begin to fear? It reminds us of Philippians 4:8, the things that are true, noble, lovely, and of good report.

Even casually reading the epistles written to Timothy, you would see that Timothy was fearful, timid, that he felt worthless to the point of tears. He even struggled with being ashamed. Note that Paul does not harshly rebuke him for his timidity, fear, worthless feelings and his shame. He gently reminds him in verse 7 that God did not give him a spirit of fear. God gave him a spirit of power and love and a sound mind.

That's the Titus 2 model. Did you notice? Paul is acting as a godly older man to a younger man, coming alongside him and teaching him how to have a God-controlled mind.

So Paul tells Timothy that he has nothing to be ashamed of. He had a great upbringing. His father might not have been very helpful, but his mother and grandmother were godly. Paul reminds Timothy he has a special position, he was a choice servant that God allowed Paul to personally train in Acts 16. Timothy had a special gifting, and in short, Timothy had no reason to be timid and fearful. But he was. Timothy appears to have a life-long need for encouragement to be bold and to go on serving the Lord. It's even possible that his stomach problems had to do with his timidity and fear.

But how do we apply a God-controlled mind? Timothy is a perfect example. If you are a person who feels uncomfortable around people, if you draw back from people who reach out to you, if you feel inferior to others, if you're afraid of always saying the wrong thing and that people will dislike you, then welcome to the club. One of the greatest pastors of all time was so much like you. Timothy, son in the faith to Paul, servant of the Lord to the largest church in the New Testament world was just like you.

Paul doesn't chastise him, rebuke him harshly, scold him, or tell him he was unspiritual. Rather, Paul tells him to get his mind back to Christ's control every time he starts to fear. Every time you start being anxious, or ashamed, every time you start feeling worthless, just strap on tight your helmet of salvation. All of Timothy's struggles were just part of living inside a fallen body with a flesh-influenced mind and emotions. And the solution is to make a conscious choice by faith to keep surrendering his mind back under Christ's control.

Spirit-Led

Is your godly mind troubled that God defines spiritual adultery in Ezekiel 20, particularly verse 31, as the sin of His people following the advice, the customs and the practices of the pagans instead of Him? The idols that Israel was following had to do with the pagan practices. The pagans had idols they believed affected their health, their business, their safety, their future security, and so on. And Israel abandoned God as their source of truth to understand life. They began to look at the pagan understanding of life, and they spent and invested more time getting help and counsel and direction and advice from everyone but God.

That's Israel in the Old Testament. But does it sound like anyone else? They abandoned the living and true God and started looking to idols, but it wasn't what we think of as idol worship. There were idols that had to do with the planting of their crops, with the fertility of their fields, that had to do with their own fertility in having children, that had to do with making money and doing well in business. And they saw the pagan ways and that they were so much easier to follow than the harsh absolutes of God. So this is what God said: "'For when you offer your gifts and make your sons pass through the fire, you defile yourselves with all your idols, even to this day. So shall I be inquired of you, O house of Israel? As I live,' says the Lord God, 'I will not be inquired of you.'"[43]

If you're getting all your help and guidance and advice from the idols, God says, you're not going to get any from Him. Our world spends most of its time seeing life through its own eyes. Our media looks at life through human eyes, and today, more and more believers are finding their world-view, their values, and their guidance for life from television, from books, from unsaved professionals, and commercials and the internet. Sadly, they follow that ungodly direction rather than God and His word. It's almost become a last resort for believers. Oh, does God have something to say about that? I'd be interested in that too.

This should greatly trouble us, if we have the mind of Christ.

Sophronedzo, the verb form that's used in Titus 2:4 for older women means that the godly older women of the church are to come alongside younger women and bring them to their senses. To restore them to moderate, self-controlled, Spirit-led living so that they are not carried away. Getting carried away by everything that comes along is the opposite of *sophron.* And we are not supposed to be like that. We are to have an anchor, that's the Word of God.

To live a life that is *sophron* is to live a life that is Word-filled and serious about spiritual things, to be God-controlled and seeing life clearly, and to be Spirit-led instead of being carried away by every wind that blows. A person who is word-filled will examine their life to see if anything is crowding out the supremacy of the word of God in their daily life. A person who

---

43 Ezekiel 20:31

is God-controlled is constantly running what comes in through the grid of what God says is worth thinking about. And a person who is Spirit-led lives their life according to what the Spirit of God breathed out in His word, not what the world, the flesh, and the devil say is worth pursuing. How are you doing? Are you a woman of God who can be described as *sophron*? If not, it's time to come to your senses and see the battle that is raging for your mind. Give that ground over to the control of God, and what comes into and comes out of your life will be defined by this incredible quality God desires for every member of His Church. Let us make that our prayer today.

God, I pray that You would accomplish Your will and Your desire in Your Church. I pray that You would cause each one of us to think about whether or not we are consciously, day by day, hour by hour, moment by moment, yielding back our minds to you. I pray that You would point out to us the human reasoning, the human understanding, the human view, the fleshly response in the mind, and instead renew our minds so that they would be Word-filled, God-controlled, and led by Your Holy Spirit. Help us to take every thought captive to the obedience of Christ, by Your grace and through Your Spirit. And in the name of Jesus Christ, whose mind we are to have, we pray. Amen.

Respond to Truth

If the God who loves absolutes were to test my mind, would He find it under His control, or under the influence of something else? What does He say about my mind (Matthew 6:24)?

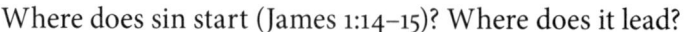

Where does sin start (James 1:14–15)? Where does it lead?

Do things that used to shock me seem normal to me now? Am I finding myself entertained by what used to offend me? What personal choice did David make about the things he saw and heard (Psalm 101:3–4)?

Is my world defined for me by God and His Word or by modern media? Do I find myself working to make God's Word fit around what I already believe, or do I believe what I hear based on whether or not it fits with God's Word?

What practical steps can I take today to pursue a Word-filled, God-controlled, Spirit-led mind (See Romans 12:2.)?

Women of Purity | *10*

When Paul first wrote this passage in a letter to Titus two thousand years ago, he was writing against the backdrop of Roman culture. Several ancient writers, whose writings are still in existence today, described how women dressed in the Roman culture of Paul's day, and that culture was the driving influence both in Ephesus, where Paul wrote to Timothy, and in Crete, where Paul wrote to Titus.

"That they admonish the younger women to love their husbands, to love their children, to be discreet, chaste."[44]

BEAUTY IN THE SIGHT OF GOD

The word "chaste," or "pure," depending on your translation, means a moral, sexual purity. And nowhere is this heart attitude more evident than in a woman's dress, and in Paul's day, the apparel of the world was very far from God's desire for women of grace.

Juvenal, a first-century Roman writer, pictured everyday life in the Roman empire, noting that women were preoccupied with their appearance. Another writer explained that this preoccupation was driven by the most famous people of the day. For instance, the wife of Caligula, one of the

Roman emperors, had a dress that was covered in emeralds and pearls and was worth over a million dollars by today's standards.

The rich of Paul's day often wore dresses that cost 7,000 denarii, or twenty years' wages for an average factory worker. Can you imagine how disruptive it was to a church service when someone walked in wearing nearly a lifetime of earnings for the majority of the people there? That's why James, in James 2:1–9, warned not to give these golden, glowing clothes-wearing rich people preferential treatment, and Jesus tells His disciples in Luke 20:46 to avoid being like the scribes, who "desire to go around in long robes, love greetings in the marketplaces, the best seats in the synagogues, and the best places at feasts."

The biblical standard is for believers to be un-entangled in, un-conformed to, and un-in-love with the world. The God of the Old Testament commanded His chosen people, "according to the doings of the land of Egypt, where you dwelt, you shall not do; and according to the doings of the land of Canaan, where I am bringing you, you shall not do; nor shall you walk in their ordinances."[45] And what was Israel's sin, the one that led them into captivity? "They mingled with the Gentiles and learned their works."[46]

And guess what? The God of the New Testament, who hasn't changed, who is still holy and who still demands purity from His people, has the exact same standard. "I beseech you therefore, brethren, by the mercies of God, that you present your bodies a living sacrifice, holy, acceptable to God, which is your reasonable service. And do not be conformed to this world, but be transformed by the renewing of your mind, that you may prove what is that good and acceptable and perfect will of God."[47]

"Do not be unequally yoked together with unbelievers. For what fellowship has righteousness with lawlessness? And what communion has light with darkness? And what accord has Christ with Belial? Or what part has a believer with an unbeliever? And what agreement has the temple of God with idols? For you are the temple of the living God. Therefore, 'Come out from among them and be separate, says the Lord. Do not touch what is unclean, and I will receive you.' Therefore, having these promises, beloved,

45 Leviticus 18:3
46 Psalm 106:35
47 Romans 12:1–2

let us cleanse ourselves from all filthiness of the flesh and spirit, perfecting holiness in the fear of God."[48]

Hagnos, to be chaste, pure, sanctified, is what we are striving for. It is our aim to be like Christ, not to be like the world around us. And the more Christ-like we are, the more we stand out against a godless culture. And to that end, Paul writes to Timothy that women are to "adorn themselves in modest apparel, with propriety and moderation, not with braided hair or gold or pearls or costly clothing, but, which is proper for women professing godliness, with good works."[49] Why? So that they would not be like the rich women of the day who would walk into church with their wealth proudly on display through elaborate hairdos with expensive jewelry woven into them.

The Bible never forbids braided hair or gold, pearls, or high-quality clothing. Both the bride of Solomon (Song of Solomon 1:10) and the Proverbs 31 woman (verse 22) wore beautiful clothes and jewelry. But God does forbid wearing those things for the wrong motives.

Both Paul and Peter explain that a godly woman ought to attract attention by her godly character, not her physical beauty. That's why Paul instructs Timothy that women are to adorn themselves with proper clothing. The word "adorn" is the word *kosmeo*, that has entered into our English language as the word "cosmetics," and the basic idea of this Greek word is "to arrange," "to put in order," or "to make ready." So in fact, Paul is saying that women should get ready for a worship service by wearing proper clothing. She should be "well-ordered" by wearing what is proper.

The Greek word translated "clothing" goes far beyond just what a woman wears. It speaks of how she wears it. Just from this verse we see that women should come to church already prepared, not in disarray either in demeanor or wardrobe. And while what a woman wears matters, it is the heart attitude and motivation behind what she wears that is the real issue. External adornment, Paul says, reflects a woman's heart.

So what do your choices in clothing say about your heart? Here's a test: Do my clothes reflect the beauty and grace of womanhood? Do my clothes show my love and devotion to my husband? Do my clothes reveal a

---

48   2 Corinthians 6:14–7:1
49   1 Timothy 2:9–10

humble heart devoted to worshiping God? Or, do my clothes call attention to myself? Do they flaunt my wealth and beauty?

So if flaunting my wealth or my beauty or drawing attention to myself or drawing the eyes of men are all the wrong motivations, what motivation does God want behind my choices for how I dress?

Paul sums this up in 1 Timothy 2:9 with two words, "modestly," and "discreetly." This is how the dictionary defines modesty: "Having a regard for decencies of behavior or dress; quiet and humble in appearance, style, etc.; not displaying one's body; not boastful or vain; unassuming; virtuous; shy or reserved; chaste."

"Modestly," in Greek, means modesty mixed with humility. It connotes a sense of shame, not to be ashamed of being a woman, but to be ashamed to ever dress in a way that incites a man to lust or that distracts from the worship of God.

Secondly, the word connotes rejecting anything displeasing to God. Some commentators note that it means a sense of grief over sin. The grace-energized woman hates sin so much that she will avoid anything that can produce sin in others. She will seek to avoid being a cause of temptation.

BIBLICAL MODESTY

Nancy Leigh DeMoss opens her article "Does God Really Care What I Wear" with this quote from one college student's letter to the editor in his college newspaper:[50] "The landscaping around campus looked exceptionally great. There were new dorms, new faces and unfortunately, scantily clad females everywhere as well. This is… particularly hard for males because they are stimulated by sight. Now guys, we are not off the hook just because females are dressed inappropriately. We are called in 2 Timothy 2:22 to 'flee youthful lust and pursue righteousness, faith, love and peace.'

50   Nancy Leigh DeMoss, "Does God Really Care What I Wear," http://www.oneplace.com/ministries/revive-our-hearts/read/articles/does-god-really-care-what-i-wear-11819.html, quoting Phillip (Freaky) Howle, "Women's choice in dress leads men to stumble," *The Skyliner (North Greenville College, Tigerville, SC), September 4, 2002.*

However, girls, help us brothers out.... Please consider your clothing and what the Bible says concerning the way you dress."

It appears that many young women do not understand what their clothing choices can do to a young man. One of the differences between the way men and women are wired mentally is that men respond rapidly to what they see, while women are more responsive to what they feel. When a woman ignores the impact her clothing choices can have on a man, she is placing an intentional stumbling block before men. Time after time, we hear of married men who fall for the flirtatious, immodest seductress at work. Is that man at fault for committing adultery with a sensual, immoral woman? Absolutely he is at fault, but so is she equally at fault for luring him onward by her clothing choices.

This problem is not new. Richard Baxter, a Puritan church leader, poet, hymn-writer, and theologian, wrote, "Though it be [the men's] sin and vanity that is the cause, it is nevertheless your sin to be the unnecessary occasion.... You must not lay a stumbling-block in their way, nor blow up the fire of their lust... You must walk among sinful persons, as you would do with a candle among straw or gunpowder; or else you may see the flame which you did not foresee, when it is too late to quench it."[51]

When God's Spirit inspired Paul to call every woman of grace to modest purity, it was because for all the generations of the church, women walk through life like they are carrying a candle among straw or gunpowder. Once a fire starts burning or an explosive charge is set off, the potential for damages, injuries, and destruction is huge.

Melody Green wrote this in an article to all born-again women on her website "Last-Day Ministries": "Unfortunately, it seems that many Christians are lost in their own selfish little world—either oblivious or uncaring about the effect they have on others. I know, because... I have done it—partly in ignorance, but mostly in rebellion.

"I can remember thinking, 'Well, it's not my fault if they can't keep their eyes off me and on the Lord. They just aren't spiritual enough. Why should I have to change just because they are weak?'

---

51   Richard Baxter, *A Christian Directory in Practical Works, vol. 1 (London: George Virtue; reprint ed., Ligonier, Pennsylvania: Soli Deo Gloria Publications, 1990), 392.*

"But the Lord showed me that it was my fault. I was responsible for causing my brother to stumble and it had to change. Once I really saw the damage my selfishness was doing to others and to the Lord, I was really ashamed of myself and embarrassed that I had been representing Jesus in such an unbecoming way."[52]

What does not seem provocative to a woman can be absolutely defeating to a man, and no woman of grace would want to become a lustful image in a man's mind. No godly woman would want to make a struggling man, seeking to walk in the Spirit, stumble instead and fall back into old temptations, lusts, and sin.

Paul's words in Titus 2:5 are a challenge from God to every woman to choose clothing that reflects the glory of God. His weight is to be felt on every choice we make, whether it's what we do with our hands, where we go with our bodies, or the clothes we put on. "Therefore, whether you eat or drink, or whatever you do, do all to the glory of God."[53]

PURE AS HE IS PURE

"Chaste," to be sexually, morally pure. That is God's desire for His Church, but the church that received Titus 2 was living in a very cosmopolitan culture. It was incredibly advanced and incredibly immoral. The sheer level of sexual temptation that assaulted the believers at every level in Paul's day rivals our own times. Men fed upon lust and found their sexual gratification everywhere they could, and women obligingly gave them plenty to lust after and became willing participants in every type of sinful behavior.

It's interesting that when Paul makes lists of things, like in Romans 1, the sin he mentions right at the beginning, almost always first or second, is sexual sin. That's for good reason. The early church was immersed in a flagrantly sexual culture. The believers of Paul's day were being squeezed by the world around them to not resist, but to just float along with the culture of self-expression, self-gratification, and lust.

---

52   Melody Green, "Uncovering the Truth About Modesty," http://www.melodygreen.com/Publisher/Article.aspx?ID=1000008635.
53   1 Corinthians 10:31

Purity is the moral quality that has always marked genuine believers in all centuries of the Church. Paul was clearly telling Titus that God's expectation in an immoral and lust-filled Roman world was absolute purity.

This is God's desire for every woman, regardless of her age. This is what girls were to be taught by their mothers from a young age, this is what younger women were to be taught by the godly older women of the church, and this is what those older women would have mastered in order to be qualified to sit down with a younger woman and discuss God's desires for her life.

God is very serious about purity and holiness. He uses those words interchangeably throughout the New Testament to describe the sanctified life He demands from His children. Purity is a description of believers who are allowing God to sanctify their lives.

The word that Paul uses, translated "chaste" in Titus 2:5, is used over three hundred times in various forms in the New Testament. That's how important it is to God. It's the same root word, used in eleven different forms, all across the New Testament, and it encompasses every New Testament reference to holiness, purity, sanctification, and saints. Sometimes it's *hagios,* sometimes it's *hagiosune, hagiazo,* or *hagiazomai,* but they're all forms of this word that mean holiness or purity that's accomplished by sanctification.

James said, in no uncertain terms, that believers are to keep themselves "unspotted" by the world.[54] As the first New Testament writer, James was warning the church even in its earliest days that the cesspool of the world that they lived in called them to make conscious choices about purity or they would become contaminated by the world around them.

Hebrews 12:14 is a very strong call God makes to all believers. He says, "pursue peace with all people, and holiness, without which no one will see the Lord." Holiness is that purity that we're talking about, that Titus 2 says is to become a conscious choice. Without the work of sanctification, without God's righteousness, without God's holiness that salvation brings to a life, there's no evidence that the person is regenerated. You won't see God if holiness is not at work in your life, if the Holy Spirit is not operative within you. God's Word says that believers are being sanctified or they're not really believers.

---

54 James 1:27

Let me give you a quick reminder of what sanctification is. As we were saved only by the accomplishment of Christ's sacrifice on the cross, we live each day by faith, the same faith by which we were saved. We are always dependent on Christ's gracious death on the cross that saves and keeps us. The grace that saved us is the grace that changes us, and God, by our trusting in Him, through the power of the Spirit, changes us to be more like Him.

This process began the instant we were converted and does not end until we meet Jesus face-to-face. There is no one who has arrived. How did Paul put it? "Not that I have already attained, or am already perfected; but I press on, that I may lay hold of that for which Christ Jesus has also laid hold of me."[55] That's sanctification.

Have you ever stood and peeled a potato? They start out brown, rough, with little dark rotten spots and bumps and everything. That's what I think of when I think of sanctification, because I love how that brown, ugly, bumpy potato gradually turns white as you peel away the skin. Through the work of the Holy Spirit, through the power of His word, and through fellowship with other believers, God is progressively peeling away our desires for sin.

"Chaste," that Paul uses in Titus 2, *hagnos,* to be sanctified, means that we are supposed to spend our lives making conscious choices to be more Christ-like. If you don't understand sanctification, that's what it is: the lifelong process of becoming more like Christ. It's the same word John uses in 1 John 3:3 when he says that a believer "purifies himself, just as He is pure."

That, in its simplest form, is what *hagnos* means. Even a child can understand that we are to be like Christ. Do you want to know how? Ask yourself, would Jesus watch that? Would Jesus go there? He might go somewhere and proclaim righteousness, but He wouldn't go there and enjoy unrighteousness. It's all about Jesus, what He would do, what He would say.

This purity, this Christlikeness, affects every choice we make, whether it's the thoughts we think (Philippians 4:8) or the things we

---

55 Philippians 3:12

do (2 Corinthians 7:11, 1 Timothy 5:22). And if you are a believer in Jesus, *hagnos*, purity, isn't just something you should have. It is who you are (2 Corinthians 11:2).

When James described the wisdom that is from above, he said it is first pure, then "peaceable, gentle, willing to yield, full of mercy and good fruits, without partiality and without hypocrisy."[56] But did you notice what is first? When the Holy Spirit is operative in a believer's life, when the wisdom from above comes upon us, we are first "pure."

God renews our minds, He changes our lives, but sanctification is about our own choices and behavior. It involves work. It's not, "let go, let God," I do nothing, God does it all, there's the potato peeler, and if He wants me peeled, He'll do it. No. Sanctification is me cooperating with God's work in my life. We are to strive. We are to fight sin. We struggle, we wrestle, we agonize. We study the Scripture. We don't just absorb it by osmosis just because we're around church. We pray. We flee temptation. We press on. We are to run hard in the pursuit of holiness. We are actively at work, engaged, and making choices all along the way. The Christian life is not easy, but God never commands us to do something that He has not already given us the grace to accomplish.

"No temptation has overtaken you except such as is common to man; but God is faithful, who will not allow you to be tempted beyond what you are able, but with the temptation will also make the way of escape, that you may be able to bear it."[57] God always makes a marked, lighted exit door. He always makes an avenue, a way, a doorway, an opportunity to escape. He personally opens the door for us to get out. He wants us to stay pure. Christ's Church has been called to a very high standard, but we have been empowered by the Holy Spirit to stay morally pure.

Believers have faced sexual temptation at every intensity level through the centuries and by God's grace have found the strength to resist. From Joseph fleeing Potiphar's wife in Genesis 39 to Paul charging Timothy to do the same and flee youthful lusts in 2 Timothy 2, God's desire for His children is clear.

56 James 3:17
57 1 Corinthians 10:13

Jesus explains that it is impurity of thought that leads to impurity of action in Matthew 15. This moral purity starts with our minds given over to the Lord and allowing God to sanctify us. The Puritans used to put it this way: "The wagons follow the ruts." What they meant by that is that a person does not just launch into some form of sexual immorality. They have thought about it, they have made pathways toward it in their minds. The ruts in the mind, the epinephrine trails through their neurons, if you want to put it that way, have led toward that fantasy or desire and their bodies will follow. The wagon follows the ruts.

Peter uses the word *hagnos* to describe our choices to be different from the godless culture, and that it is this, this purity, that is our testimony to them of the power of God. When you're around a godless person, even if you're married to them, they will see something in you that is different, and it should be this purity.

"Wives, likewise, be submissive to your own husbands, that even if some do not obey the word, they, without a word, may be won by the conduct of their wives, when they observe your chaste conduct accompanied by fear."[58]

Saint Francis of Assisi said that we are to preach Christ always, and if necessary, we are to use words. That's what Peter's saying here. Even if you don't say a word, this holiness that God calls for is so powerful when it stands out against a godless and sexually charged culture that even if they are disobedient to the word, either unbelievers or believers who are in disobedience, they are often won over when they see *hagnos* in your life. That is a powerful testimony.

Just your conscious choices in the area of purity, to not be squashed and led along and drift with the godless culture, is a powerful testimony to the power of salvation. Why is this such a powerful thing? How can this one characteristic, when people witness it, win them to Christ? Because of how different it is from the culture.

God calls us to be chaste, to conduct ourselves like the holy servants of God that we are. Don't give in to your culture. Don't reflect the sexual liberty and license of your day. Stand for purity. Keep yourself

---

58   1 Peter 3:1–2

pure for Christ's sake. Learn the gracious art of living a pure life, and be a role model that Christ can use in the Church.

OUTWARD REFLECTION OF THE INWARD CONDITION

God may look, not on the outward appearance, but on the heart,[59] but God very much cares about the clothing we wear. Why? Because our choices in clothing reflect what is in our heart, and a heart devoted to God will express itself in the clothing we wear, or our clothing will betray a heart that is not devoted to the purity that God desires from His people.

First, our clothing is to reflect Jesus Christ. "Let us walk properly, as in the day; not in revelry and drunkenness, not in lewdness and lust, not in strife and envy. But put on the Lord Jesus Christ, and make no provision for the flesh, to fulfill its lusts."[60]

If we are to be wearing Jesus Christ figuratively and spiritually, shouldn't that impact the things we actually wear? In Titus 2:5, the Apostle Paul asks whether each woman is really acting and living and dressing like she is clothed with Christ.

If Jesus were here now, actually doing His itinerant work, how would people describe what He looks like? Do you think Christ would ever choose to dress in a way that was provocative, sensual, or revealing areas of His body that God's Word says need to be covered? Do you think He would ever choose to appear skimpily attired, with sexually arousing outfits? Do you think Jesus could ever be described as hot, immodest, alluring, or edgy?

These words, which should only ever be used to describe unsaved, unbelieving, worldly people, now describe everyone, Christian and not. They've crossed over because many Christians think "under grace" means "not under sanctification." Not under holiness, purity, or biblical modesty. But Titus 2:12 tells us what "under grace" really means. It means that we now have a tutor that teaches us to deny ungodliness, whether in thought, in action, and yes, even in the way we dress.

---

59   1 Samuel 16:7
60   Romans 13:13–14

What would a woman clothed with Christ on the inside wear on the outside? How would she reflect Christ? Would a woman clothed with Christ wear something on the outside that causes godly men to look away?

John MacArthur, in his book *Different by Design,* says, "The tragic number of pastors who have fallen into immorality indicates that not all women in today's church have entirely pure motives." But "if you are focused on worshiping God, you won't have to worry about how you dress because your commitment will dictate your wardrobe."

Our clothing should, secondly, reflect God's ownership of our bodies. First Corinthians 6:19–20 says, "Or do you not know that your body is the temple of the Holy Spirit who is inside you, whom you have from God, and you are not your own? For you were bought with a price; therefore glorify God in your body and in your spirit, which are God's."

We are not just to glorify God on the inside, with our heart attitude, in our spirit, which belongs to God. He bought us with a price, all of us, including the outside, and what we put on our bodies is a reflection of the Person who has taken up residence inside us.

Have you ever thought about how much you can tell about a person by looking at the house they live in? If the lawn is kept in perfect order and the house is maintained, you can guess at the type of person who lives there. But if the paint is peeling and the weeds are growing and the roof is caving in, somebody very different lives there.

If a woman goes around inciting men to stumble by the clothing she wears, who do you suppose lives there? The Holy Spirit of God, who bought her with a price?

In her book, *Uncovering the Truth About Modesty,* Melody Green says, "Our bodies are precious because they are a gift from God. They are attractive because God made us in His image for His pleasure (and if we are married, to please our mates as well). But God never intended us to flaunt ourselves or exhibit our bodies in an immodest way (Romans 12:1). Many Christians are either oblivious or uncaring about the effect they have on others. They may even appear to have a real excitement and love for the Lord—however, their body is sending out a totally different message."

We have been invited by our holy God, the One who dwells in unapproachable light, as Paul said in 1 Timothy 6:16, to become the very dwelling place of God. Imagine that for a moment. Just that, the companionship of God at the instant of our salvation, coming inside us, making us His dwelling place. And His only request is purity. That we keep the body that He's dwelling in, His temple, the place He lives, clean. That's the essence of purity. We are living, walking temples of God, He wants us to make sure that temple is reflective of the holiness of the God who lives within, and what we wear is a reflection of whether or not we are the pure and holy temple of the infinite, immortal God.

Thirdly, our clothing should reflect what is worn in heaven. Whenever we see someone in heaven described in Scripture, whenever someone is coming down from the presence of God, what do they look like? What characterizes them?

The look of heaven is the look of purity, modesty, holiness, and a priest-like reverence. Every time an angel's clothing is described, it is described as befitting someone who just came from the presence of God. They look like big, strong men, but they wear long garments. "And entering the tomb, they saw a young man clothed in a long white robe sitting on the right side; and they were alarmed."[61]

When the saints are pictured in heaven, worshiping God, they are described as "standing before the throne and before the Lamb, clothed with white robes, with palm branches in their hands."[62] Jesus Himself, when He appears to John on the island of Patmos, is described as "One like the Son of Man, clothed with a garment down to His feet and girded about the chest with a golden band."[63]

When you walk through modern-day gatherings of young people, it would appear that no one has let them know that God invented clothing for the sole purpose of covering His creations after the fall. When Adam and Eve sinned, they were convicted of their sin, and sewed fig leaves together to cover their nakedness. When God saw their attempt, He fashioned better coverings for them out of animal skins.

61 Mark 16:5
62 Revelation 7:9
63 Revelation 1:13

God covered their bodies because they were ashamed; they knew that they were uncovered. Part of the fall was the sinful lusts that manifested themselves and God provided a way to help deal with those sinful lusts by inventing clothing specifically to cover.

God declares in Titus 2:5 that His plan for your life is purity. Will you follow His plan? Will you surrender your life? Will you let Him make you a grace-energized woman of purity? In each generation of Christ's Church, God has been looking for women who will give themselves to His plan for their lives. When women offer themselves as willing servants to follow God's plan, His grace energizes them to live a life that magnifies Christ at every level.

Purity is not getting a checklist and following it, and if you do this and this and this, you're alright. Biblical modesty is not a dress code. It's a heart code. It is choosing to be clothed with the humility that never wants to draw attention to itself, that is not showy or distracting, that reflects worship instead of distracting from it. It is choosing to be clothed with the modesty that is ashamed to ever be a source of temptation or lust to a Christian brother. And it is a choice to reflect our Savior, reflect the Holy Spirit who lives inside us as a pure temple of God, and to reflect the holiness and purity seen in heaven and by those who come from God's presence. It is a choice to feel the weight of God's glory on every choice we make, from our actions to our thoughts to our clothing and everything else in life.

Dear heavenly Father, I pray that in all of our lives we will choose to reflect You. Your priorities, Your character, Your holiness. That we would reflect to a watching world what is holy and pure before You. And I pray that when it comes to what we wear, we will make choices that honor those around us as those trying to follow God and keep their eyes on Him. May those choices extend to every area of purity in our lives and that the holiness that we reflect becomes attractive to a lost and dying world. In Your name we pray and for Your glory, amen.

Respond to Truth

Even more than my words, what does God say is the most powerful witness to a godless culture (1 Peter 3:1–2)?

Does God care about my outward appearance or dress? Does my appearance send out a message that is different than what is in my heart (1 Timothy 2:9)?

Does my clothing show a devotion and love for my husband? Does it reflect my commitment to worship God? Or do my clothes draw attention to me, show off my beauty or my wealth, or tempt the men around me?

Has God put a young lady in your life that you can come alongside as a godly older woman and encourage her to be a woman of purity?

11 | Pursuing Homemaking in a World Filled with Homelessness

Job 39 tells us the ostrich has no wisdom or understanding and therefore does not even care for its own young offspring. Proverbs contrasts the wise and the foolish woman. In Proverbs 14:1, God warns that a foolish woman tears down her own house. Anyone can build a house, but a woman of godliness builds her home. She builds carefully, intentionally, with wisdom and love from God above.

So what is homemaking? Homemaking gathers all parts of life into its arms. A homemaker builds, organizes and maintains a home that welcomes, receives, refreshes, nourishes, protects, instructs, listens, understands, encourages, mends, equips, forgives, trusts and loves her husband, children, and all who enter there. Balancing the care and order of all the needs of the people in your home is a monumental task! Home is where the love of God is learned and lived.

God has a high opinion of homemaking. The primary nurturers of the souls of the next generation are not the youth pastors or the Sunday School teachers, or even the pastors or the elders. God designed mothers to be the primary nurturers. The forging ground of the souls of the individual followers of Jesus Christ was never primarily the corporate gathering. It was to be the home, the nurturing center where a godly father and mother talked about God when the children rose up, when they sat at meals, when they walked through the day, and when they went to bed at night. A pastor or Sunday School teacher spends only a few of every week's 168 hours with that child. For the other 165 or so hours, it is the wife and mother who has the greatest influence over her family. And that nurturing Christian home is fast facing extinction.

GOD'S CALL TO WOMEN

We're about to look at probably the most disputed word in Titus 2:3–5: "homemakers." Just that one word, translated as "homemakers," "keepers at home," "to be busy at home," or "workers at home," was designed by God as the role-specific ministry that pleases Him. This sums up what God wants for godly women who offer their lives to Him through their ministry to their home.

The very concept of "homemakers" is increasingly offensive to our twenty-first-century world. To say that the Church was to be regularly deploying the very best of the best, the godliest of the women to trickle through the congregation and train the younger women to be home-makers—it sends a shiver through our society. It's so antiquated, so out of place in our culture today.

In many households, both parents work, sports become top priority, and electronic devices take over people's lives, so home life has been reduced to a house where detached minds and disconnected people live spiritually and emotionally compartmentalized lives.

To this detached era of church history, God continues to offer the Christian home, guarded, nurtured, and filled with Christian love, as a godly woman's highest priority, but of all the godly traits God asks for in a grace-energized woman, homemaking is the most controversial. Husband-lovers? Even the world says we could use more of that. Children-lovers? If you ever see a mother mistreating her child in the mall or the supermarket, you know that our society expects us to love our children.

But to be a homemaker? In our liberated-woman, egalitarian society, nothing is more offensive than the homebound slaving woman that this passage seems to portray. Even in the Church today, nothing is harder than to convince wives that their primary ministry is their husbands, and mothers that their primary calling is to disciple and nurture their children. But this is the call that God sent throughout His church of the first century.

The church at Crete who received this letter to Titus was saved out of a very unspiritual culture, and even though they were saved, they still had clinging to them the ideals of their culture, just as we do today.

But whether our culture agrees or not, whether it's easy or hard to do, whether others obey or not, God is looking for women who see their home as their priority. They first love their husbands with an emotional friendship that we've already seen, they love their children with nurturing love that is always kind, and they see their home as their God-given priority. Grace energizes us to live differently from the culture, no matter how good the wisdom of this world sounds.

Did God Mean What He Said?

In our culture that values independence and individualism and the liberated woman, it's easy to look at these commands as an outdated concept from centuries ago. But if we take Paul's scriptural instructions to women as being biased because he was Jewish in his upbringing, or we look at them as antiquated because of his culture, if these words are no longer binding, authoritative, or relevant, we come up with a bigger problem.

If Paul's position was biased or in error or only locally for those people in that time, then it calls the rest of Scripture into question as to whether it's authoritative, inspired, and trustworthy. If Paul can't be trusted in his teaching on women, did he get other parts wrong in the half of the New Testament that he wrote? If Paul was wrong about women, who knows if what he says about men, and how men can be saved, is correct? Those who dabble in this selective interpretation of Scripture may solve the minor problem of women who don't obey these commands by saying they're not binding, but they face the much larger problem of the authority of Scripture and the very basis of our faith and our hope of salvation.

I firmly believe that every word that Paul wrote was under the inspiration of the Holy Spirit, and thus totally trustworthy. Yes, there are some issues that Paul addressed that may have been local and cultural, such as the exact nature of the head coverings in Corinth, but he never mentions that issue anywhere else, and because of very specific things that were happening in that place and that time, and because God's people are to set themselves apart from the world and everything it stands for, Paul did address a local, cultural issue. But no good interpreter of God's Word can say that about God's instructions on the role of women. They are not vague. They are specific, and they are repeated and supported across God's Word from cover to cover.

To seriously question Paul's instructions to women is to seriously question the authority of God's Word. And one of the clearest biblical teachings directed to the Spirit-prompted women of all times is that they, if married, are to be busy at home. This desire of God is seen consistently from Genesis to Revelation. This is His desire, this is His design, and this is what His grace energizes us to do.

Following God's Design

When Saul, who would become Paul, was on the road to Damascus, and God shone down and knocked him off his horse, do you remember what God said? "It is hard for you to kick against the goads."[64] God was saying, "I have something specific for you to do, and when you don't do it, it hurts."

The same thing happens to us as believers when we don't follow the plan that God has laid out for us. What's so fascinating in life is that people struggle and just can't make it and can't figure out why, and often it's because they're out of step with what God wants them to do, what God walks through life giving them the grace to do what He designed them to do, and what He wants them to succeed in doing.

God's plan is always best. Think of the joy that it can be to go through life doing exactly what God designed you to do. What God wants you to do. Think of the joy of walking through life as God gives you the grace to

---

64 Acts 9:5

help you succeed. That is what a grace-energized homemaker has to look forward to.

If God's plan is always best, then what is His plan? Well, marriage for a believer brings men and women into definite, God-ordained roles. When you get married, you instantly click into God's design, into a role that God has created you for, and a married woman who is a believer must make a conscious choice to obey the Lord and make her priority of life to be her home. If you are a believer, and you are married, you know exactly what God wants you to do. He wrote it down, clear as day. That the younger women are to be taught to be "homemakers."

The word "homemakers" is a compound word: *oikourgos.* It comes from two Greek words, *oikos,* "house," and *ergon,* "work." But what's fascinating is the Greek word for work isn't just to work. It denotes specific job focus. It's not just being out there in the working class. It's someone who knows what they're supposed to do and they do it.

This is the word the New Testament uses for strategic, spiritual ministry. It's used throughout the New Testament for those who had a specific job, role, task that the Lord gave to them.

When God asks a grace-energized woman to focus on her God-ordained role as a homemaker, He asks her to join in with a ministry that is strategic to God's plan. It's not that the men are all over here doing something spiritual and the women are over in the corner doing the dishes. No. This is crucial to God's plan for His Church. God looks at things in a different way from how we do. Under the power of God's Spirit, by using this word, *oikourgos,* Paul elevated what could be thought of as mundane to the level of strategic ministry.

A grace-energized woman believes that God has called her to do the work of homemaking by and for the Lord Himself. She's not called by her husband to do this. And it's not for her husband. It is a calling by the Lord and she accomplishes it for the Lord.

In John 4:34, Jesus uses the same word, *ergon,* "work." This is what Jesus was called to do, and how He described it. Jesus declared His specific, focused ministry when He said, "My food is to do the will of Him who sent Me, and to finish His work."

Jesus looked on His earthly life as a specific plan, a role, a position, a ministry, a job, a focused task that was given to Him by God. He said the same thing on another occasion: "I have glorified You on the earth. I have finished the work which You have given Me to do."[65]

Now, Jesus' work is very different from ours. His was the work of reconciliation, which we could never do, but the point is that He was doing what God called Him to do. That's why He was so pleasing to the Father. And you and I can also be pleasing to our heavenly Father when we follow God's plan, when we do the specific focused work that He designed us for.

God clarified the focused work of the church in Antioch when He said, "Set apart to Me Barnabas and Saul for the work to which I have called them."[66] It wasn't that going out and getting beat up and thrown into jails and walking endless hours on those Roman roads and getting into shipwrecks was just the thing they did. They had a purpose, a specific, focused ministry that God planned for them, and they were obedient to it.

Paul explains the focused ministry of his fellow worker, Epaphroditus, in Philippians 2:30: "Because for the work of Christ he came close to death." He did what God planned for him to do. In 1 Thessalonians 5:13, we are called to esteem the elders of the church "very highly in love for their work's sake." If they stay with the program, if they stay on track, if they follow the plan, if they do the specific, focused work that God calls them to, they are to be highly esteemed and God is well pleased.

Does that make you look at Titus 2:5 a little differently now? God isn't relegating women over to a corner to do housework because somebody's got to do it and the men are busy with the spiritual things. He uses the same word that Jesus does when He describes what God sent Him to do. The same word that God used to call great missionaries like Barnabas and Paul into the mission field. The same word that Paul used to commend Epaphroditus when he nearly died to accomplish it. The same word that makes elders worthy of high esteem. This work that God calls godly women to is specific, focused, and vital to His kingdom.

---

65   John 17:4
66   Acts 13:2

Redeeming the Time

Homemaking is looked down on by our culture, but it is looked upon very highly by God. Your view of homemaking shows who you're listening to. If you think it's demeaning or beneath you, then you're listening to a voice other than God's.

Through each day of the past twenty centuries, God has offered to every woman the privilege of turning each moment that she spends working in her tent or her apartment or her palace or wherever she is into eternal crowns that she will someday cast at Christ's feet.

Think of what exactly God is offering: each dish that you wash, each diaper that you change, each towel that you fold, each day that you spend serving your family can become worthy of eternal reward that will never pass away.

Titus 2:5 promises each grace-energized homemaker that she can redeem every moment she spends in the endless duties of the home as an offering of obedience to God. Isn't that the most wonderful offer of redeeming the time possible?

You can be as great a servant of the Lord as it's possible to be in this life by living out your God-given priority of loving your husband and your children in a home you have embraced as your priority.

WHAT GOD SAYS ABOUT THE ROLE OF WOMEN

Before we look at what God means by homemakers, let's start with what it doesn't mean. When Paul wrote the Holy Spirit's instruction that married women are to be homemakers, he was not saying that they could do nothing else.

That's just our human nature to do that to God's Word. God says in the Garden of Eden that they're not to eat of the tree of knowledge of good and evil, and when Eve tells the serpent what God said, she goes even further. We can't eat it, or even touch it. But God didn't say that. And God doesn't say that a woman can do nothing else but housework.

It's so easy for us to embellish, to enlarge, what God says, but God never said they can't leave the home, that they can never be active outside the home, or that they can never have a career. That's never in the Bible. Some Christian books, maybe, but not the Bible.

In fact, one of the favorite passages for mothers, especially on Mother's Day, is Proverbs 31:10–27 on the godly woman of virtue. And one of the facets of this woman's life, verse 16, is the purchase and management of real estate investments. And in verse 18, she appears to have a small manufacturing business. She makes items with her hands and sells them. So there's nothing in Titus 2 or anywhere else in Scripture that says being a homemaker is relegating a woman to doing nothing else but housework.

Another misapplication of God's instructions is that a woman is to do all the work at home. This is a classic one that men love. There's a whole generation of men who have rarely touched a dish, rarely changed a diaper, rarely lifted a finger around the house. "You're the homemaker; I don't touch that." Now, I don't think it's because of the Bible, I think it's because of laziness, but there are Christians among them who really believe a wife is called to do all the work at home.

But in fact, as the God-ordained head of the house, the husband is called to lead by Christ's example. And Jesus came, not to be served, but to serve. So as the head of the home, the husband is not to be served in that home, but to serve. He is to follow Christ's example as head of the Church, how He served even to the washing of His disciples' feet.

The chief servant is to be the husband. A godly husband will lead the way with a servant's heart as Philippians 2:7 says, and all the time giving honor to his wife, as 1 Peter 3:7 says, as to a weaker vessel. Not that he's strong and she's weak, but that he's weak, and she's weaker. And the husband, understanding that, will be assisting his wife in every way he can as a servant leader.

So firstly, to be a homemaker does not mean the wife can do nothing else. Secondly, it does not mean that she does all of the work of the house. And thirdly, it does not mean that she is in any way second-class to men.

I think it bears much repeating how highly Paul actually spoke of women. Think about it: The same Paul who wrote 1 Corinthians 11:9 ("Nor was man created for the woman, but woman for the man") also wrote Galatians 3:28. "There is neither Jew nor Greek, there is neither slave nor free, there is neither male nor female; for you are all one in Christ Jesus."

God teaches gender-specific roles in the home (Ephesians 5), and in the Church (1 Timothy 2), but God's Word just as clearly declares absolute spiritual equality in Christ. There is no spiritual higher ground that men have on women. The spiritual standing, spiritual access, and spiritual position that we have in Christ is one of absolute equality. No question. Some people put men too high. Some people put women too high. But if you just use the Bible, you see an absolute equality between men and women in a spiritual sense.

The gender-specific role God ordained for women does not mean she can't work outside the house, that she has to do all the work in the house, or that she is in any way second class to men. But just as God's Word teaches that men and women are equal, it also teaches that they are given different roles by God.

"Let a woman learn in silence with all submission. And I do not permit a woman to teach or to have authority over a man, but to be in silence. For Adam was formed first, then Eve. And Adam was not deceived, but the woman being deceived, fell into transgression. Nevertheless she will be saved in childbearing if they continue in faith, love, and holiness, with self-control."[67]

Paul says that a woman's role in the Church is as a learner and not a leader or teacher. That is the gender-specific role of godly men. But her God-ordained, gender-specific role, is to spiritually follow God's desire to manage a home built around faith, love, and holiness. She finds her greatest blessing and complete fulfillment from God, and she gets the privilege of rearing children who are God-hearted, useful servants. The men who teach and lead in the context of the Church, only teach and lead for an hour or two a week. The women completely control the curriculum, nurture, and discipleship of their children the rest of the week. Any married woman who resists being a grace-energized homemaker works against the divine plan established by the God of the universe.

---

67   1 Timothy 2:11–15

Not only does God define a woman's role in the context of the Church, but also in the context of the home. "That they admonish the young women to love their husbands, to love their children, to be discreet, chaste, homemakers, good, obedient to their own husbands, that the word of God may not be blasphemed."[68]

Do you notice the priorities that God gives to women? First, her husband, second, her children. Of the seven qualities God is looking for in grace-energized younger women, four have to do with the home. The first two He lists are dictating what a woman's priority should be. She is also to be a homemaker, verse 5, and the last quality God is looking for is for her to be submissive to her own husband.

Any married woman who wants to do God's will makes her home her priority. That's what God's Word says. That is what God means by "homemaker." God demonstrates that He allows a great deal of freedom in how this is done (see Proverbs 31), but what is vital is that the priority of the home is heeded.

Any marriage and home where this priority is neglected is headed for serious problems. No one can violate a specific directive from God without consequences. "Do not be deceived, God is not mocked; for whatever a man sows, that he will also reap."[69]

Think of two women, both believers, both wanting to serve the Lord, but so different. The first is always on the move from ministry at church to volunteering at school. She sings in the choir, shuttles her children everywhere, attends two Bible studies, and teaches Sunday School. She is always on the go. Her husband has asked her to stay home more and keep the home from becoming a disaster, but the one thing she never does is stay at home.

The other woman is the opposite. She's home most of the time. She is lazy, watches TV, sleeps in, and often lets her children get up and get ready for school themselves. At night, she's rarely tired, stays up reading or watching TV, but never gets done any of the projects that she agreed to do. Her husband has asked her to get up, help the children, and get her work done.

---

68   Titus 2:4–5
69   Galatians 6:7

Both of these situations are typical among women who know the Lord: the superwoman who is everywhere and does everything but stay home, and the anything-but-super woman who stays home and never seems to get anything done. Both need to stop and examine their lives to see where they have diverged from God's plan.

God's plan is for grace-energized women to *oikodespoteo,* guide or rule their house. Wives who are gone from home too much with activities or work can't guide or rule their house. Similarly, wives and mothers who are always home but are not "busy at home" are equally disobedient to the clear command of God to guide or rule their homes as well.

If you are a married woman, here is a quick checklist to determine if you are either away from home too much, or if your priorities while at home are not being guided by God's Word.

- Am I often too tired to plan and cook meals or keep the house orderly?
- Am I constantly feeling the pressures of never having enough time to finish what needs to be done?
- Is my husband often stressed or troubled by things not getting done on time?
- Do I find myself feeling irritated at my children because I am stressed or tired?
- Am I always wanting to eat out and never at home?
- Because of the pace of my life, am I no longer able to show hospitality or even entertain my friends at my home?
- Am I slowly losing interest in my homemaking responsibilities?

God's Word calls us to question our priorities, to see if they line up with His expressed priorities for us. And if they don't, to begin taking steps to get back in line with His plan for our lives.

Being a godly homemaker is so much more than just whether you're physically inside or outside of the building you live in. The measure of this virtue is not whether you work outside the home or not. God's call to women is not so much that their place is in the home. It's that her priority is for her home.

God's Word teaches that the home is a woman's special domain and that it must always be her highest priority. It is within the home that a woman can provide the best ways to express her love for her husband and children, and thereby obeying the Lord and following His plan. The more she believes that, embraces that, and cultivates that, the more her priorities are focused around her home, whether or not she is physically standing inside the walls of the tent or apartment or wherever she lives.

Examining our priorities is only the first step. God also calls us to examine our motives. When a wife is working, or considering entering the workforce, she needs to examine what claims God's Word has made on her choices. And one of the best ways to make the choice about whether to work outside the home or not is to sit next to a godly older woman and honestly answer some heart-searching questions about what is prompting you to work outside the home.

- Is it because I desire more material things?
- Is it because I'm tired of the constant demands of caring for my children?
- Is it to make myself an independent woman who is secured by her career?

None of these reasons, after careful examination, are God's plan for a grace-energized woman. God's plan is for a woman to be content where He has placed her (Philippians 4:11), to be grateful for the possessions she has rather than always wanting more (1 Thessalonians 5:18), and to stay home as much as it takes to maintain a haven of truth and love for her family (Titus 2:5). And all of this is for the glory of God (1 Corinthians 10:31).

A woman doesn't have to physically spend all her time in her home to be a godly homemaker, and a woman who spends all her time at home isn't necessarily the homemaker God calls her to be either. God says, not that a woman's place is the home, but that her priority is for her home, and a grace-energized homemaker will seek to make her priorities line up with God's, examining her motives for everything she does.

PURSUING GOD'S DESIGN

Practical Homemaking

God has two guidelines for a grace-energized homemaker, two specifics that He says He's looking for and will reward. The first is that she sets the tone for her home.

"The wise woman builds her house, but the foolish pulls it down with her own hands."[70]

The word the Holy Spirit of God breathed out in this verse doesn't just speak of the physical structure of the house. It also speaks to the reality that a house is for the people who live in it, and that it is to be built into a home. And who does God say is supposed to shape that home for her family?

Much like the thermostat regulates the temperature of your house, a grace-energized homemaker sets the emotional and spiritual temperature of the house. When words get heated in the house, a godly woman can give a soft answer that turns away wrath, as it says in Proverbs 15:1. When hearts turn cold, a godly wife and mother becomes a conduit of encouragement, exhibiting a merry heart, encouraging with a cheerful countenance as in Proverbs 15:13. This, of course, is impossible to maintain humanly. That is why only a woman energized by grace can maintain a godly atmosphere in her home.

The second guideline God gives to homemakers is found in Proverbs 31:27. "She watches over the ways of her household. She does not eat the bread of idleness."

The word used here for "watches" is very descriptive. Literally, it means to "hedge about," like a mother bird would do to protect her young. This reminds a godly woman that her assignment from God is to watch over both the house and the people in it. "She does not eat the bread of idleness," implying that constant care is involved. The meals, the schedule, the clothes, the health and so much more is watched, guarded, and done as an offering of worship to the God who called and assigned this highest of duties.

---

70   Proverbs 14:1

God's Plan for Single Women

The role of homemaking in Titus 2 is defined as being for married women. This admonition comes to a woman who has already been commanded, as a wife, to love her husband, and, if she is a mother, to love her children. So obviously, she is married.

But what about all the women who are not married? Who may never be married? Is there no place of special favor and ministry for them?

Often it is hard for singles to be around marriage-focused fellowship. They feel left behind, left out, or even cheated. This can lead to withdrawal, isolation, morbid introspection, and loneliness. Unchecked, all of these responses lead to growing anxiety, frustrations, and bitterness. That is not God's plan.

My favorite example of God's plan for single women is a woman named Henrietta Mears. She guided Billy Graham as he started his crusades. She actually trained Bill Bright as a college student in her classes, and she was at his house when he founded Campus Crusade for Christ.

Later in life, Dr. Mears testified that she had met a man who did not have a personal relationship with Christ, but he wanted to marry her. She waited, prayed, and believed that God wanted her to fully seek and serve Him. And she couldn't do that with this man. After him, no man seemed to fit in her heart, and at the time, she recorded this prayer:

"Lord, You have made me the way I am. I love a home, I love security, I love children, and I love him. Yet I feel marriage under these conditions would draw me away from You. I surrender even this, Lord, and leave it in Your hands. Lead me, Lord, and strengthen me. You have promised to fulfill all my needs. I trust in You alone."[71]

At the end of her life, Henrietta testified to God's grace. She described how the Lord gave her more in every way than she ever dreamed. Through her Sunday School ministry, she had thousands of children who loved her, thousands of children she poured her life into. She said that from the day she surrendered her future to the Lord with that prayer she never looked back, and God never ceased to open the doors of ministry, family, and friendship for her.

---

71 Ethel M. Baldwin and David V. Benson, *Henrietta Mears and How She Did It (Ventura, CA: Gospel Light, Regal Books, 1966)*, 42–43.

Even though God presents marriage and family life as a major way to fulfillment, it isn't the only avenue. God has designed a road of blessing for every person who surrenders to His will and will follow Him through life. The greatest step is enjoying supremely through life the unwavering companionship of Jesus Christ, the only One who can go through every moment of our lives together with us.

Accepting God's Plan for my Life

Whether married or single, with or without children, a grace-energized woman sees that God has a plan for her life, and whatever it is, she accepts it as from Him, for her, as a part of His design.

Grace-energized homemakers first understand that their calling is from God. This isn't something society demands, or the husband demands, or that a woman is backed into because someone has to watch the kids and the husband is working. This is a calling from God, and managing her home is what God believes is best.

"And do not be conformed to the world, but be transformed by the renewing of your mind, that you may prove what is the good and acceptable and perfect will of God."[72] Once our minds have been renewed by the Word of God, once we see that it is God's design, desire, and command for a woman, if she is married, to manage her home, it becomes so much easier to love what God wants done, and what once was thought of as tedious becomes the sweetest offering of worship we could offer to God.

"And whatever you do, do it heartily, as to the Lord and not to men, knowing that from the Lord you will receive the reward of the inheritance; for you serve the Lord Christ."[73]

When God's grace helps us resist the pressure of the culture, when we set our minds on His plan and His will, then we live out God's best. And God's best, for a married woman, is the home management that pleases the One who called her into this ministry. She can be as great a servant of the Lord as it's possible to be when she surrenders to God's plan for her. And when her homemaking is done, not as a chore, but as if it's being done for

---

72 Romans 12:2
73 Colossians 3:23–24

Christ Himself, whether she's changing diapers, washing dishes, or doing the laundry, she is earning rewards that will never fade away. And every moment spent in doing what God calls her to do, with the attitude of offering it as worship to God, is never wasted. What an incredible offer.

> *Lord, we accept Your offer today. Whether we are single or married, men or women, we want to accept Your very best into our lives. I pray especially for the workers in the home, for those You have graciously allowed to have that most precious responsibility to their husbands and children, that You would enable them to see the blessings and the benefits of following Your plan. Let them see that the way of the world may be flashy and convenient, but it is not what is best, because You, O Lord, know what is best. You see us and You made us and we are, in Your image, made to be a certain way. And I pray that we will embrace that for ourselves as Your path of greatest blessing. In Your name we pray and for Your glory, amen.*

Respond to Truth

Does my opinion of homemaking more closely resemble the world's opinion or God's? What parts of God's plan for a grace-energized homemaker have I been neglecting?

How does God define the biblical priorities of a grace-energized woman (Matthew 22:36–37; Titus 2:4)? Does my daily schedule reflect those God-given priorities? What practical change can I make today to follow God's priorities for my life?

How would I describe the atmosphere in my home? What am I doing to regulate the tone of my home? How does that compare with God's design for a home? (See Deuteronomy 6:5–9.)

Am I such a perfectionist that I am always dissatisfied with my home and can't enjoy it with my family?

Are the menial tasks I do done for my husband? My children? Or as an act of worship to God? What in my life would change if I saw each task as an offering of worship to Him?

Is my home ruled by electronic devices, or endless activities? Or do I create a hedge around my family, guarding what comes in so that the focus is God-honoring? What in my house and schedule distracts from a God-centered home, and what steps can I take to "watch over the ways" of my household?

Grace-Energized Women of Kindness | 12

Someday, when our journey on earth ends and we stand before Christ's throne, there is one word that will describe what God will eternally reward. That scene before Christ's throne is well-known to us from 2 Corinthians 5:10, where Paul captures the eternal moment we have lived our lives on earth to prepare for.

"For we must all appear before the judgment seat of Christ, that each one may receive the things done in the body, according to what he has done, whether good or bad."

Did you catch the word? The one word that God uses to describe every motive, every thought, every action, every decision in life that so pleases Him that He says it's worth keeping forever? The word is *agathos,* or "good." When the Holy Spirit of God inspired Paul to write this word, it means something very specific, something that God is looking for in every generation of His Church. When used of everything but people, it simply means "good," but when used for a person, *agathos* means "kind." It is a person who is characterized as generous, benevolent, gentle, tender-hearted, and merciful. This is what I call grace-energized kindness.

Titus 2:4-5: "That they admonish the young women to love their husbands, to love their children, to be discreet, chaste, homemakers, good."

Everything that we do, if it is not characterized as "good," if it is not prompted by grace-energized kindness, is going to burn someday.

Have you ever thought about the words the Holy Spirit chose to describe people in the Bible? Every time a person in Scripture is described as good, the Spirit of God that breathed out that word, *agathos*, to describe that person isn't just throwing out a random description. God is commending that person. He's pointing them out, saying, "That right there is what I'm looking for."

In the whole New Testament, only four people are described with this word. Just four. They lived in such a way that the Holy Spirit pointed them out saying, "That's what you should be living like." When they stand before the judgment seat of Christ, they are eternally rewarded for what they did because it was good.

The first person described as "good" in the New Testament is in Luke 23:50. Joseph of Arimathea sacrificially gave his family tomb to Jesus and publicly identified with Jesus by burying Him. All it says about him is that he was a good man. That's it.

We know a little bit more about Dorcas. Acts 9:36 describes her as "full of good works." Isn't it interesting that of all the women in the New Testament Church, the Holy Spirit would choose this one to praise as being good? Why? This woman was known as a generous, loving servant of Christ's Church. She served in real and tangible ways. God's Word talks about the coats she made and how she provided for others. Many people testified as she died of her kindness and generosity. She was described as a woman whose works benefited others. She did charitable deeds, acts of kindness, and she spoke words of kindness.

The next one is found in Acts 10:38. "God anointed Jesus of Nazareth with the Holy Spirit and with power, who went about doing good and healing all who were oppressed by the devil." I think it's fascinating that Jesus' entire ministry was summed up by this one word. He was sent by God, anointed with the Holy Spirit and with power, but you know what it doesn't say? He went around raising the dead and walking on the water and feeding thousands? No. When the Holy Spirit comes with power upon a life, it is described as *agathos*. Jesus went about doing good. He was kind, tender-hearted, gracious, and generous, and what He did was good.

The last one is in Acts 11:24. As a pastor, it's fascinating to me who God chooses to be pastors, and the qualifications He's looking for. And this is a description of Barnabas, the pastor of the first Gentile church: "For he was a good man, full of the Holy Spirit and of faith. And a great many people were added to the Lord."

Barnabas had a simple life of kindness. He was sent from Jerusalem to pastor the first great missionary church at Antioch. He was a Hellenistic Jew, born and raised on Cyprus. He was from the Greco-Roman world, not from Jerusalem, but he was closely watched by the elders in the church at Jerusalem. And you know what they saw? If you remember from Acts 4, when there was a great need, he sold his property on Cyprus and gave the money to the apostles, so they respected him for his godliness and generosity.

Barnabas was also a great encourager. He could be described as cheerful, big-hearted, and loving. He was the perfect choice for the pastor that was needed. The church at Jerusalem, the mother church if you will, looked out at this mushrooming Gentile church in Antioch, and they realized they had to send out a pastor for that assembly, and they immediately thought of Barnabas.

So this generous, big-hearted, encouraging man who brought along the Apostle Paul, who had done great and mighty things for the Lord, was sent out to the church at Antioch. And when he arrived, Acts 11:23 says, "When he came and had seen the grace of God, he was glad, and encouraged them all that with purpose of heart they should continue with the Lord."

Barnabas had eyes to see the evidence of the grace of God. Do you know what grace-energized kindness does to an individual? It changes how they look at life. Barnabas is a crucial character in the New Testament. He's the first pastor, that we know of, of a Gentile church. He was sent to a people steeped in sin, filled with paganism, and that didn't have a biblical background in their culture. Remember, the Jewish people knew all this whether they believed it or not. This is the first time non-biblically-oriented people were gathered together as a church, and who did the the elders at Jerusalem send? Barnabas.

Grace-energized kindness causes you to look past the exterior. Barnabas could have easily seen the situation in a different light. These people were new. They were untaught Christians. He was the first teacher they'd ever had, so they knew nothing of the Christian life. They had just gotten saved, they were caught up in the excitement of the moment and they were brand new. They were still carrying the mire of Antioch with them. They had miles to go in their language, in their relationship, in their ethics. But Barnabas saw the evidence of the grace of God. He saw Christian grace and charm in their lives, the fruit of the Spirit, love, joy, and peace.

Instead of focusing on how far they still had to go, he focused on how far they had come. "He was glad," it says, and he simply encouraged them to remain true to the Lord with all their hearts, to meditate on Him, and to make Him everything. In this way he helped them focus on what would cleanse them from the defilement of Antioch, and his advice is relevant to all Christians, whether in the beginning stages or well along the path. As the great preacher McClaren said, "Many of us are so busy thinking about Christianity that we've lost our hold of Christ." So Barnabas just encouraged them to hold on to Jesus Christ.

Do you know someone like that? Why not be a person like that? A person who sees life through grace-energized kindness. The result is seen in verse 24. The goodness and faith seen in Barnabas began to reproduce, and a great number of people were brought to the Lord.

What's amazing is that, yes, Barnabas was a great teacher and discipler, but his personal life was characterized by being loving and gentle and kind and generous and encouraging. And that is what God is looking for in His people.

GOD'S WANT AD FOR WOMEN

Imagine for a moment if God gave you a stock tip. If God, who knows everything, who has all future events factored in, and who knows all the secret thoughts of all involved, were your stockbroker, and He called you and gave you an investment tip, would you respond?

That's exactly what God gives us. God says that His Church should invest heavily in kindness. If a woman who has this quality ever wanders by, grab her, invest in her, support her so all she can do is this. This ministry of kindness is so vital and strategic for God's plan that He tells Paul that it's actually something he can use the offerings of God's people to invest in. You want an investment tip from God? This is it. This is what He points out as so valuable, He's placed a want ad for it where all can see.

I remember in the old days they used to have, in the grocery stores, those papers with all the tabs on them, and you'd tear one off if you wanted to buy the person's car or boat or something. You'd put a want ad up if you were looking for something. Well, God has placed in Titus 2:5 a wanted poster. He is looking for grace-energized kindness. The context is that Paul is asking Titus to train women in the church to be kind in their personal life, kind in their marriage, kind in their home life, kind in the way they minister to others in Christ's name. But in this verse, all he gives us is the word "good." It's vague. How do we, with God's Word in our hands, understand what it is that God is looking for. What does a life of "good" works look like?

If God says that this is His measuring stick for our eternal rewards, then He must quantify it and clarify it for us. We can see this quality in everyday life by looking at what Joseph did, and what Dorcas did, and what Jesus did, and what Barnabas did, but what does God want you to do? We saw a man who was good, but how does God ask women, who can't lead a church like Barnabas did, who can't be a pastor teacher like he was, to live in a way that is good? What qualifications is God looking for in His want ad for women?

In 1 Timothy 5:10, Paul publishes a job description. This is where God has posted His want ad for women, and He actually gives five qualifications for the women He is looking for. In fact, the context of this verse is that God is telling the Church who they should support. Paul said there are certain women, who, if you see them and they meet these qualifications, you should support them on the spot. Pay their way so they can do this because it's so valuable and priceless for the Church. If they're a widow, the Church should eagerly support them so that they can continue in this grace-energized kindness that God says is so valuable.

No matter where you are in life, this is what God wants you to be as a wife, as a mother, as a single woman in the Church. This is what God has placed on His want ad, what He is looking for. He has advertised in His Word what He's looking for, and it is found in 1 Timothy 5:10.

"If she has brought up children, if she has lodged strangers, if she has washed the saints' feet, if she has relieved the afflicted, if she has diligently followed every good work."

What exactly marks one of these good women? What exactly are their qualities that impressed God? What draws His special interest and attention? God asks for five areas of your life to be surrendered to the control of the Holy Spirit. In summary, grace-energized women of kindness are intentionally family first, purposefully hospitality-conscious, prayerfully humble servants, compassionately Good Samaritans, and energetically devoted to ministry.

Intentionally Family First

Grace-energized women of kindness see their family as their first priority from God. "If she has brought up children." This lines right up with everything in Titus 2, that a woman's first priority is her home. If you have a husband, he's your family, and if you have children, that's more of your family. A younger woman is to be trained, number one, to be a lover of her husband, and number two, to be a lover of her children. That's Titus 2. And it's the first good work of this woman of renown that God has placed His want ad for.

If this were a job interview, this would be the first question to see if the woman is qualified for the job, if the Church were considering supporting her. What kind of mother are you?

Are you faithful to your home? Based on your high calling to be a homemaker, is your home your priority? Do you watch over your home and the people in it as part of your special assignment from God? Are the meals, the schedule, the health, the clothes, and so much more treated as an offering of worship to the God who called and assigned these as your highest responsibilities?

Is your tongue characterized by kindness toward your children? Are you a Proverbs 31 mother who, Proverbs 31:26, raises her children with the law of kindness on her tongue? Are your words kind, encouraging, gracious, and gentle like Christ's? This is the same word, *agathos*. And for a woman who is family first, *agathos* rules her tongue the same way it rules everything else.

This woman looks past her culture, her peers, and realizes that God says her priority is family first, so she decides she's going to do that. She doesn't let anyone else assign duties to her if God has already assigned her family as her highest duty.

Notice it isn't church first. It's family first. If you neglect the family, your word isn't credible in the church. Even the elder, if he is not watching over his home and caring for them in a way that is orderly, he cannot have a valid testimony for God. So for a woman who wants to be valuable in God's kingdom, with a reputation for good works, who God says is worth investing in, family is her highest priority.

Purposefully Hospitality-Conscious

Hospitality? Is that even spiritual? We think of knowledge and study as making us spiritual, but hospitality is actually a qualification for elders, ranking right up there as a sign of a mature Christian.

Hospitality is not entertaining. The word means "a lover of strangers." It's consciously seeking out, more and more, people who are not connected to the grace of God in a meaningful way within the fellowship of Christ's Church and intentionally going after them.

This woman is on the prowl, looking for ways to do the biblical priority in ministry of hospitality. The verse says, "lodged strangers." We would warn people not to lodge strangers. Don't pick those people up by the road. They might mug you. Right? And there is wisdom in that, but this is talking about in the context of the Church.

This woman of kindness is supposed to "lodge strangers," and that's another way of asking how she used her home. Her home is, first, her priority, and now the question is how she used her home. When your God-given priority of caring for your family is done, do you offer your home to be opened to ministry to others in an unselfish way? Are sacrifices made to serve others through your home for Christ's sake? Do you use your home as a ministry tool?

Hospitality to strangers is a quality God esteems so highly that He made it one of the clear qualifications for elders in Christ's Church.[74] The Church is to look for elders who reach out and try to welcome in strangers and get them connected into the body. This is also a mark of spiritual maturity.[75] And Paul says that older women in the faith are to train younger women how to use their homes in a godly, hospitable way for strangers.

Who are strangers? In the context of 1 Timothy 5:10, it's those not yet connected and nurtured in Christ's Church. They're out there seeking and they want to know the Lord, they've come to know the Lord, and they're not quite yet connected and nurtured. And this woman is always looking for ways to make her home a connecting and nurturing place in Christ's Church.

Our society is increasingly becoming individualistic. Because of our cultural obsessions with privacy, this makes everyone a stranger at times. For believers, we are called to community, to be different. A grace-energized woman who manages her home is also the gatekeeper for hospitality. She sets the tone for her home. Peter explained that this is one of the ministries that a grace-energized homemaker can engage in.

"Be hospitable to one another without grumbling."[76] We are not only to love one another (previous verse), but we are to love strangers. That is literally what the word "hospitable" means, to love strangers.

Hospitality is going extinct in our individualistic culture, but grace-energized homemakers see that God's will for believers is to open their homes and welcome in those they do not know, and extend to them the love of Christ.

This is not an invitation to enlarge your guest list for entertaining more of your friends at your home. Sometimes our entertaining can become a source of pride. We find ourselves wanting to impress our guests with the beauty of our home so they can look on with admiration. Entertaining

---

74 1 Timothy 3:2; Titus 1:8
75 Romans 12:13; Hebrews 13:1–2; 1 Peter 4:9
76 1 Peter 4:8

is ashamed of those old Formica surfaces in the kitchen, but hospitality doesn't need granite countertops. You can show hospitality with anything, but when you entertain, you always have to be upgrading.

Hospitality never seeks to impress. It only seeks to serve. Hospitality whispers quietly in the background to those who are served, "what's mine I share with you." Hospitality focuses on serving the person, not on the house, not on the food, not on the host. The focus is serving, not showing everyone what you have. In fact, the more you have, the prettier and more lavish and more expensive it is, often, the harder it is to show Christ-like hospitality.

The best manager of the home is a grace-energized homemaker that heeds God's calling to love Christ supremely—more than our home, more than our possessions. And one way to strengthen Christ's supremacy is to de-accumulate our possessions.

The world is constantly trying to infect us with discontent, a syndrome that drives us in a constant cycle of buying more stuff. Godly contentment and simplicity are disciplines, and godly people who are ensnared by needing more ought to simplify so that they can help many families who are in need. What's mine I share with you. That's hospitality.

Prayerfully Humble Servants

The third qualification for a woman of kindness is "if she has washed the saints' feet." The gospel was spread down the dirty and dusty roads of the ancient world, and in those times, the care of feet was a daily chore. At the last supper, Jesus used the menial task of washing His disciples' feet to demonstrate who was a servant. If you remember, they all had proud hearts and stinky feet. So Jesus took off His outer garments, put the towel of a slave around His waist, and knelt at each disciple's feet and washed them.

By the way, the towel tied around His waist is the same word that Peter captured in 1 Peter 5 when he said that elders should be girded with humility. They should be the ones who tie on the towel of a slave to go around and do the most menial, humble spiritual ministry in the lives of those who most need it. That's what grace energizes us to do. Foot-washing is not high on the list of big, public ministries. It's a quiet, humble, out-of-the-way thing, and a grace-energized woman prayerfully considers how to invest her time in humble ministry.

Notice she's not just a servant. She's a humble servant. There are a lot of servants who are not humble. A humble servant does anything they're told to do. Non-humble servants can't be told what to do, they won't be told what to do, and if they don't like what they do, they don't do it. That's not a servant. We've lost the meaning of this word. Real servants are humble. They don't have to be seen, they don't have to be recognized, they don't have to be praised, they don't have to be honored, they don't have to be stroked. They just serve Christ. And that's what this woman is.

She has a humble heart for serving others. She is Christ-like in that she comes not to be served but to serve. She is not above humble ministry. She is characterized by it. She is constantly praying and saying, "Lord, I'm doing this just for You." And if no one likes it, she does it anyway. If no one notices, she still does it just for Him. If people criticize it, she still does it. She doesn't want to be seen or recognized. She does it only for Christ.

Compassionately Good Samaritans

Fourthly, the grace-energized woman of kindness compassionately does selfless and sacrificial deeds. She has surrendered her life to be on the lookout for selfless ways to serve others. She knows that Jesus says even a cup of cold water held out to a child in the name of the Lord will never lose its reward. And for all the centuries of Christ's Church and all the cultures of this world, the Spirit of God finds these willing servants and He gives them the strength to spend their life doing selfless deeds of kindness. It characterizes them. They don't have to be begged. They're drawn toward relieving the afflicted.

This woman has the Good Samaritan heart of reaching out to those stricken with need. Remember the story of the Good Samaritan? We have busy people going down a busy highway, and the more outwardly religious they are and the more entrenched they are in the trappings of their life, they more the just scoot on by and don't stop. But the Good Samaritan stopped and, as 1 Timothy 5:10 says, "relieved the afflicted." That's what characterizes a woman of kindness.

Energetically Devoted to Ministry

The last quality of a woman of kindness is if she "has diligently followed every good work." The grace-energized woman of kindness doesn't just do ministry. She devotes herself to it. She is a fan of it. That's what it means to be energetically devoted to something.

The word "devoting" that Paul uses is a very strong word. *Epakolutheo*. It's a life lived like Dorcas, who was diligent, devoted to her ministry. These women follow every possible way to do what is good. They are fans of serving God. They talk about it. They model it. Even the flag of their life on their car or their license plate or their email address—it all points to their devotion to ministry.

They never get to the point where they say, "Well, we used to do that, but now we're at that age where you have to stop doing all that to enjoy yourself and relax." No. Grace-energized women of kindness are devoted to ministry to the end. They're Psalm 92 Christians, they just want to die serving the Lord.

The Lord God, our Savior and Redeemer, has singled out one type of individual and described her so we can spot her, and then He says she is priceless in what matters to Him. If you want to have the highest, most revered ministry in the Church, this is it.

First Timothy 5:10 is very different from a list of the who's-who of this world. Here we find Christ's "who is valuable for My Church" list. Who enriches the body of Christ in a strategic way, who helps His Church grow in godliness, grow in ministry, grow in worship. And Paul says to look for this kind of person and invest in them. They are the models to follow, the teachers to be revered. They are the women of God useful to God, rewarded by God, and these women have made five simple choices that should become the daily goal of every woman in Christ's Church.

Someday, we're going to stand before Christ, and He is going to open the history file of our life, and it's going to show our actual motivations, our intentions, our thoughts, and our actions, and there will be exposed the complete picture of what we did with our life. Anything and everything that was done for Jesus, that was done with kindness, whether relieving the afflicted or opening our home to strangers or valuing our family as our highest, God-given priority, whether it's being a fan of every kind of good work and ministry, or washing the stink and the dirt off someone's feet in humble service, all of that will never lose its reward.

Lord, we want to answer Your want ad. We want to be qualified for this, Your greatest desire for us, to be pleasing to You, wherever we are, at whatever stage of life we are in. Let us value what You value. Let us seek what You seek to see in us, and let us worship You with our lives. In Your precious name, amen.

Respond to Truth

Am I someone who can see past the exterior like Barnabas and see evidence of the grace of God in someone, or do I still see only their faults and shortcomings? What does grace-energized kindness see?

If God gave my church a stock tip, would He recommend they invest in me? Does my life show visible evidence of kindness in how I raised my children, how I used my home, in acts of humble service, in how I relieved the afflicted, and in how I devoted myself to every ministry God called me to? What is supposed to rule my tongue (Proverbs 31:26)? What causes a tongue to be ruled by kindness (Matthew 12:34; 1 Corinthians 13:4)? What does a tongue ruled by kindness sound like (Matthew 5:44; 1 Peter 3:9; James 4:11)? What does James say about anything that rules the tongue (James 3:2–5)?

Do I entertain my friends or do I lodge strangers? Do those I bring into my home feel impressed or do they feel loved? Are my possessions a source of pride and worry that need to be protected, or have I so given them over to Christ that if they are lost or ruined, it's only a blessing to use what God has given me for His Church?

If no one ever saw me serving, would I still do it? If someone tells me what needs to be done, am I eager to do it, or do I resist being told how to use my gifts for Christ?

Do the figurative bumper stickers, flags, T-shirts, and caps of my life advertise that I am a fan of God, His people, His house, and of ministry? If my friends were asked what I am devoted to, would it be ministry?

13 | The Joy of Submission

Since the Garden of Eden, there have always been two roads. Two pathways. Two choices in life. Either I pursue and seek and follow after God's way, or I pursue and seek after and follow my own way. When God looks down from heaven, He sees only two types of people. Those who are in His kingdom, and those who are in the kingdom of Satan. And God says that one of the clearest distinctions between His people and His enemies is that God's people, those He has bought from the slave market of sin and made members of His family, are characterized by submission. And the others, those who have not been redeemed and regenerated, are characterized by disregarding or throwing off of authority.[77]

The last grace-energized character quality God is looking for is that younger women be taught to be "obedient to their own husbands,"[78] and it's the most controversial of all the words we've studied so far. The word translated "obedient" in NKJV is rendered as "subject to" in both the NIV and NASB, and it means to line up behind, like an army would line up behind its commanding officer. What God asks of godly women of grace is so much more than just obedience. It's a whole attitude that begins with a woman saying that she wants to go God's way, not her own, and that is reflected in her relationship with her husband.

---

77   Jude 8
78   Titus 2:5

Much of the controversy surrounding this passage and the present-day turning-to-our-own-way that Isaiah 53:6 warns about is simple rebellion, but much of the un-submissiveness of wives to their husbands in the church today is due to a misunderstanding of what the word "submit" really means. So before we study what godly submission looks like in a marriage, let's start with what submission doesn't mean.

WHAT SUBMISSION IS NOT

Misconception #1: Submission is Only for Women

Ever since the fall of the human race, we as human beings have been characterized by one great sin. Isaiah 53:6 says it best: "All we like sheep have gone astray; we have turned, every one, to his own way." In fact, most conflicts in life come down to a competition between my way and your way, his way and her way, our way and their way. We are born, every one of us, wanting his own way, and every sin is a choice to go our own way instead of doing things God's way, the way He has laid out in His perfect Word.

Submission is not just for marriage, and it's not just for women. Each of us is to submit, first of all, to God, James 4:7, but second to each other as it says in Ephesians 5:21. Congregations are to submit to their elders.[79] Citizens are to submit to their rulers.[80] Younger believers are to submit to older or mature believers.[81] And all of this is because mutual submission is a part of God's plan.

The first twenty verses of Ephesians 5 are a description of a life that is led by the Spirit of God, and the whole culmination of the Spirit-filled life is found in the command of verse 18: "Be filled with the Spirit." And what does that look like when the Spirit's leadership starts coming out in a person's life? When we give our lives over to the control of God? Verse 21: "submitting to one another in the fear of God."

See, it's not out of fear of one another that we submit. It's not that the congregation is afraid of the elders or that the citizens are afraid of their

79   Hebrews 13:17
80   1 Peter 2:13
81   1 Peter 5:5

rulers, or that the woman, because she is afraid of what her husband might do, keeps to the background and says very little and just kind of does everything he tells her to do. No. We submit, in all the realms God has laid out in His Word, because we have a God in heaven who is holy and just and worthy of our fear, our reverence. And because we have this respect and fear of God, we obey His command to submit, first to Him, and then to each other in all the ways He lines out.

In Ephesians 5 and 6 there are seven principles, and the first and the last are the same, that we all submit to one another. But then in between it touches on all the realms of life, wives, with respect, are to submit to their husbands, husbands, to their wives by loving them, then we have children to their parents, employees to employers, employers back to employees, and then it ends with the same idea of this mutual submission that has always been a part of God's plan, and it is an essential part of the life of any woman who desires to be pleasing to God.

Misconception #2: Submission is Bondage

When God calls for biblical submission of wives to their husbands, many people hear something that God never intended, that wives are to be in bondage to husbands, but that is just as far from the perfect roles God designed as the home where the wife is completely un-submissive to her husband. Both extremes are the result of the fall.

When Satan first tempted Eve to eat of the forbidden tree, both the woman and the man departed from their God-designed roles. For the first time in human history, the woman desired to rule over her husband. She took the lead, and Adam also departed from his God-designed role as leader and protector of his wife by following her into sin. And ever since, there has been a corruption of the roles that God designed for marriage.

The fall created both, either a husband who is forceful and tyrannical, or a husband who has become passive and uncaring. We have both ends of the spectrum. And the wife, in reaction, either resists the dominant tyrannical husband or, either by default or by usurping her husband's role, has become the leader she was never meant to be in the home. This whole distortion began way back in the garden and even in Christian homes, we have husbands who have become either passive, uncaring men who are all too happy to let their wives lead the home, or they've become tyrants, and have turned biblical submission into bondage that God never intended it to be.

The way the translators of the King James and New King James rendered the word "submit" in Titus 2:5 is that young women are to be "obedient to their own husbands," but no other Bible translators used that word "obedient," and everywhere else this Greek word *hupotassumenas* is used in the whole New Testament, it's never rendered "obey." It's always "to submit," or "to be subject," but never "to obey."

"Obey" carries with it this idea that the husband snaps his fingers and the wife jumps up to do whatever he says. But that's not what the Spirit of God inspired the Apostle Paul to write. The word is so much broader than that, and it carries with it this idea that the wife is not just to obey, like a child might do, obeying on the outside but mumbling and complaining on the inside. No. She is to submit, to line up behind, to accept the role that God has designed.

There's something about submission that's often overlooked. God designed marriages so that husbands and wives see their roles in the context of a spiritual partnership of godly love and as a biblical covenant they made with God.

Paul wrote to husbands in Ephesians 5:26 and described a leadership that involved sacrificial love for the one he leads. A husband who misuses his role as leader is just as sinful as a woman who won't submit to him. We often see such relationships and say, "Oh, she's not a submissive wife." We should equally say, "He isn't Christlike. He isn't a servant leader. He isn't a reflection of Christ's love."

Submission is a choice. Husbands are never commanded to demand submission from their wives. They are commanded to win it by love. God doesn't make us obey. He asks us to obey out of love. And biblical submission is a choice that every wife has to make for herself to be obedient to God. We don't go around with the submission squad checking that every wife is subject to her own husband. It is between the woman and God, and it is a beautiful act of worship to Him. And it is a command from God, not the husband, not the friends. From God. It is a choice, and it is a choice you'll be rewarded for.

Biblical submission is not bondage to a husband. It's submission to God. A grace-energized wife submits to her husband's leadership in her life because she has already submitted to the Holy Spirit's rule in her life first and foremost. It is a reflection of the submission that Jesus Himself modeled. Remember that in all things Jesus submitted to His heavenly Father, and certainly that wasn't bondage. No. Jesus portrays submission as freedom. It frees a woman to be all that she was meant to be. And it's not done out of obligation, but out of gratitude for what God has done in our lives. It makes us happy to please Him, happy to serve Him, and happy to extend that submission to all areas of our lives, including the God-designed role of women in marriage.

Misconception #3: Submission Means Muting

Many people think that submission means that the husband has a mute button and the wife is not permitted to speak. The Scriptures that describe a godly wife never state or imply that she may not speak. On the contrary, she is to become the treasured confidant, advisor, and completer for her man who stands in front of her, protecting her, not silencing her. This is seen in Proverbs 31:26, Acts 18:26, Judges 13:21–23.

In God's plan, husbands are not to make every decision in the marriage, nor does his role as the leader make every decision a correct one. God knows that we are imperfect people, but we have a perfect God, therefore a husband should often consult his wife's opinion, or he is very foolish.

But, there are some decisions that no matter how long you discuss them, you will not agree. It is at that point that a godly wife submits to her husband's role and he leads as best he can with his understanding of God's will. This means that a godly woman must come to the place of practical submission before she gets married. Ask yourself these questions:

Husbands, are you ready to answer to the Lord for the decisions you make in which you overrule your wife's opinions and you go forward with what you think is best in that situation? You will answer to Him for your decision, because the Lord says if your wife submits to you, you are responsible for that decision you made, especially if you did not agree with her insight that she shared.

Wives, can you voluntarily submit to your husband's decision after you have shared your heart and yet you still differ on the decision? The Bible says that a grace-energized woman of submission will say yes. Because she trusts the Lord who judges rightly, and she obeys what the Lord told her to do by submitting to her husband even if she doesn't agree with what he's deciding to do.

Biblical submission does not mean muting. She gives her opinion. She gives the reasons she thinks it's a bad idea. But she is called, by God, not by her husband, to submit, and when the husband, as the godly leader of the home, makes a decision, even one she disagrees with, she is onboard from that point on.

Godly submission does not mean that there are two sides, and the wife always has to let the husband win. Godly submission means that after the decision has been made, she is fully and completely on his side. There are no longer two opinions. There is one opinion, and the wife never throws it back in the husband's face if he's wrong.

Do you see how this is different from mere obedience? Obedience kind of huffs and puffs and puts its head down and goes along with the husband's decision, but the second things start going badly, that wife says, "don't you wish you'd have listened to me?" Godly submission never says, "I told you so." Godly submission completely supports whatever decision is made, even if she disagrees with it, because she's not just obeying the husband. She's submitting to God. The husband is imperfect, and God knows that. But she serves a God who is perfect, and His plan is godly submission to her husband. So that's why she does it. Not because the husband's always right, but because God is, and this is what He asks of her.

Misconception #4: Submission is Inferiority

Submission never means and it's never implied to be inferiority. The Bible clearly commands wives to submit to their husbands,[82] but it just as clearly states in Galatians 3:28 that men and women are equal. God has made

---

82   Ephesians 5:24; Colossians 3:18; 1 Peter 3:1, 5

gender-specific roles for men and for women, but He never says that spirituality differs. He never says that access to Him differs. There is a magnificent equality in Christ. There is no spiritually closer position that the husband has over the wife or vice versa. God never says a woman is inferior in her giftedness or her ability to serve and please Him, just that there are roles that He has designed, and it's not because one is smarter or has more aptitude.

So why would a woman who may be smarter or more spiritual or have giftedness in the area of leading others choose to subject herself to this maybe unspiritual husband who doesn't want to fill God's role for his marriage? Because it's biblical. And because it's God's plan. And because she has chosen to accept God's plan for her marriage and to submit to Him.

The Scriptures never imply that a woman is anything less than equal with a man, but God has ordained gender-specific roles for the home and for the Church. In history, many women have excelled men in many areas, but to excel with God, submission equals obedience to a God-given role.

Remember Jesus' example? He was equal with God, but as Philippians 2:5–8 says, "Let this mind be in you which was also in Christ Jesus, who, being in the form of God, did not consider it robbery to be equal with God, but made Himself of no reputation, taking the form of a bondservant, and coming in the likeness of men. And being found in appearance as a man, He humbled Himself and became obedient." And because of that, God exalted Him. Jesus did nothing on His own initiative. He sought only the will of Him who sent Him.[83]

This is the example that every grace-energized woman of submission seeks to follow. This role is important to God, so it becomes important to her. This doctrine is one of the least liked in all the Church, but God blesses those who choose to honor what He values, and He values grace-energized submission.

Misconception #5: Submission is Invisibility

The implications of submission are huge. It is impossible for two people to come together in a biblical marriage and remain independent. You have to

83   John 5:30

be mutually dependent, and mutually submissive. Believers who consider marriage should always come to an understanding of the implications of biblical submission before they come together. This is one of the great discussions men and women should have before they get married. Not what does marriage mean financially and legally, but what does this mean to God. Do I see the correct role?

But the correct role does not mean that the wife is invisible. Actually, a submissive wife opens the door to endless opportunities because by obedience she frees God to give all that He wants, in His plan, to give to her. It is rebellion that holds back anyone's true potential from God.

THE PROVERBS 31 MODEL: WHAT SUBMISSION IS

Submission is not just for women, it's not bondage, muting, inferiority, or invisibility. But if those are the things that submission is not, then what does it mean to graciously submit to the husband? What does grace-energized submission look like practically in the home? This is a list of nine ways submission comes out in the life of the woman surrendered to God.

Submission Draws

A grace-energized wife draws her husband. She realizes how hard it is for her husband to live and work in the world. Temptations swirl around him all day long. Weariness and discouragement come at him from all sides. So a wise wife decides that her home will be a magnet for him, a shining beacon on a hill that beckons her husband to come home.

The home becomes the place he would rather be when he is at work or at play. It is his place to refocus and be refreshed and renewed. The grace-energized wife is the guardian of that place. When activities and the urgent overrun this priority, the home needs to be reset to the place of refuge her husband needs. As it says in Proverbs 31:11, "The heart of her husband safely trusts her; so he will have no lack of gain."

Submission Pleases

"She does him good and not evil all the days of her life" (Proverbs 31:12). What man can resist this kind of woman? She has a lifelong desire to do what pleases him.

Of course, wives are still, first of all, believers, so God would never ask them to sin or dishonor Him by fulfilling their husband's wishes.[84] But any wife who loves God offers herself in every possible way to willingly be her husband's helper, completer, and companion, one who delights him at all times.

Submission Honors

A grace-energized woman of submission also honors her husband with her words, attitudes, and actions. "Let the wife see that she respects her husband."[85]

Only the Lord has a higher place for this grace-energized wife. No house, no job, no child, no ministry can hold her; she wants to please and honor the man God made for her. This is her calling and role given to her by God Himself.

Submission Blesses

A grace-energized woman of submission blesses her husband. The Lord said that our words flow from our heart. That means that a godly wife, full of the Holy Spirit, would never speak wickedly to her husband or about him to other people. She gives her mouth to God and meditates upon this verse: "She opens her mouth with wisdom, and on her tongue is the law of kindness" (Proverbs 31:26).

"Let no corrupt word proceed out of your mouth, but what is good for necessary edification, that it may impart grace to the hearers… And be kind to one another, tenderhearted, forgiving one another, even as God in Christ forgave you."[86]

Submission Serves

A grace-energized woman of submission serves her husband. A grace-energized wife directs the house, the children, the schedule, and the meals to make her husband's life a joy.

84 Acts 5:28–29
85 Ephesians 5:33
86 Ephesians 4:29, 32

"She watches over the ways of her household, and does not eat the bread of idleness. Her children rise up and call her blessed; her husband also, he praises her: 'Many daughters have done well, but you excel them all'" (Proverbs 31:27–29).

The reason the Proverbs 31 woman was so amazing is that her marriage was at the center of all that she did. It was her primary ministry.

Submission Forgives

The woman of Titus 2:5 is to submit to the man of Titus 2:2 who has already repented of anything that would be seen as unfaithful, impatient, or tyrannical, but it doesn't mean that those things are gone forever. We are to be characterized by repentance, constantly going to the throne of grace and confessing our sins and receiving forgiveness. And forgiveness is the same way. We forgive. And we forgive again.

A submissive woman is characterized by forgiveness, not by holding it over her husband's head that he's messed up one more time. No. Submission forgives, seventy times seven, or as many times as it takes.

"Love suffers long and is kind; love does not envy; love does not parade itself, is not puffed up; does not behave rudely, does not seek its own, is not provoked, thinks no evil; does not rejoice in iniquity, but rejoices in the truth; bears all things, believes all things, hopes all things, endures all things. Love never fails."[87]

Christ's love causes a grace-energized wife to forgive her husband's failures, weaknesses, and struggles. God's grace allows her to look at him with eyes of love and to think the truth. Her motto is to love him as Christ loved her.

Submission Waits

Many wives are miles ahead of their husbands and can get so frustrated at their plodding. Don't discourage your husband. Don't push him. Wait for him.

"Walk worthy of the calling with which you have been called, with all lowliness and gentleness, with all longsuffering, bearing with one another in love, endeavoring to keep the unity of the Spirit in the bond of peace."[88]

---

87   1 Corinthians 13:4–8
88   Ephesians 4:1–3

Do you remember what 1 Peter 3:1–2 says? "Wives, likewise, be submissive to your own husbands, that even if some do not obey the word, they, without a word, may be won by the conduct of their wives, when they observe your chaste behavior." You know what that says? Wives, don't preach to your husbands. Don't nag them. Don't keep reminding him. Pray. Let the Lord do it. You don't need to.

Submission Trusts

If you are married, it is God's will. And since it is His will, you need to trust God with the details. The Lord can get your husband to shape up in an infinitely greater way than you ever could. All the Lord asks is that you trust Him with your husband. So what should you do? Trust your husband as God's man for you for life.

"Be anxious for nothing, but in everything by prayer and supplication, with thanksgiving, let your requests be made known unto God; and the peace of God, which surpasses all understanding, will guard your hearts and minds through Christ Jesus."[89]

Submission Inspires

A grace-energized wife inspires her husband. Husbands can't resist godly wives. That is what Peter said. So, maintain a spiritual devotion to God. A dynamic, ongoing relationship with Christ is the key to being enabled to lovingly and respectfully submit to your husband's leadership.

WHAT SUBMISSION DOES

Submission Multiplies the Blessings of Marriage

At weddings, a unity candle is often lit to signify the two lives becoming one. First, two outside candles are lit, and then the center candle is lit and they extinguish their own candles. The problem with many marriages is that they still act like they have two candles. Two lives, two goals, two

---

89 Philippians 4:6–7

directions, two plans. God says they're supposed to be merged. And what happens when a couple is merged together by the beautiful role of submission that God has designed?

Submission multiplies the blessings of marriage. Remember Genesis 2:24, where the two become one? This merging is a public declaration that all the gifts and talents and strengths and goals and hopes and dreams and desires of two lives are poured into one vessel. The result is the multiplication. Each positive facet of each of the partners is poured together and the result is that it multiplies.

But the other side of this is that everything that is lacking is also poured together and is reduced greatly. When you get married, you pour all your weaknesses in, and when they are shared, they are lessened. And when you pour all your strengths in, they are multiplied.

Submission Draws a Couple Closer

Not only does submission multiply the blessings of marriage. It also draws a couple closer. First Peter 3:7 says that husbands and wives are "heirs together" of the grace of life. Submission opens our lives to each other. A godly wife gets to share every part of the life of the one she loves most on earth. That is what Paul said in Ephesians 5:24. "Therefore, just as the church is subject to Christ, so let the wives be to their own husbands in everything."

When wives willingly accept submission and husbands gently give them loving consideration, they are both in submission to Christ. They're both following His example. They both enjoy God's best and His plan in their marriage. And anything less than that shared in mutual submission leads to a marriage that misses out on God's best. It produces a spiritual life robbed of God's blessings and growth.

The grace of life in 1 Peter 3:7 may refer to the opportunity to have children. They are certainly a gift from God, Psalm 27:3. But it does not exclude couples who have no children. They are still promised spiritual riches if they obey God's plan for their marriage.

Submission Liberates a Woman to be
What God Designed Her to Be

When we see submission as God designed it to be, we are amazed. It is not a dungeon. It is a delight. It is not bondage, but liberty. It is not a bitter pill to swallow, but a lifelong meal prepared for us by the Creator: "My food is to do the will of Him who sent Me, and to finish His work" (John 4:34). Did Jesus just dutifully obey? No. He delighted in obeying His Father. And when we truly submit, we also delight.

Biblical submission is vital to godly living. And it's not just an action. It's an attitude of humble living. If you look at the James 4 passage, right after it commands us to submit to God, it says to humble yourself. Submission requires an attitude of humility that permeates everything we do. When the Bible says to clothe yourself with humility, it does not mean a facial expression. It is a willful submission, a conscious submission to the one in authority, and a joyful acceptance of God's rule.

Why is grace-energized submission so important? Look at Titus 2:5. "That the word of God may not be blasphemed." When this submission is absent, or when any of the other characteristics of a grace-energized woman are absent, God is not glorified by that woman. God is not glorified by that marriage. God is not glorified by that home. God is not glorified by that church. But that's not all. His word is discredited. When wives don't love their husbands, when mothers don't love their children, when women do not submit to their husbands, then God's word is blasphemed.

As we live out our marriages and our personal lives, we are before a watching world, and we either point them to an awesome God, or we give them ammunition to use against God and against us. Either we live out a gracious picture of God in this world or we give ammunition to the critics.

God is mocked when we do not live how His Word commands us to live. For the world to be convinced that God can save them from sin, they need to see people living holy lives. Before you can interest someone in the sweet by and by, they need to see God at work in the here and now. A godly marriage is a picture of Christ and His church, and for a wife to be un-submissive to her husband is to give the world a picture of a church that is not living in submission to our awesome God.

On the other hand, there is a gracious work of God that happens in a woman's life when she submits to her husband as to the Lord. When she models her life after what God says is important, and when she makes that life an example that others can follow. A woman is not liberated by independence from her husband. She is liberated when she no longer fights against the beautiful role that God designed for her, but instead embraces it as the pathway to God's best, both for her marriage and for her life. Such a life not only glorifies God, but produces a peace and joy that only complete submission to the will of God can provide. Let us all seek God's best in our lives and in the roles He has designed for us in marriage.

Dear Father, this prayer is not just for the grace-energized women of the church, but for all of us, Your servants. May we be filled with the submissiveness of Christ, who emptied Himself and poured Himself out to take on the dress and role of a servant. Who obeyed You even to the point of death, and who honored You with His obedience, and so You honored Him. Let us submit, first of all, to You, O Father, and then as we see our God-given role in marriage and in the Church, that we would submit to each other as You designed it. Let us find the joy of submission daily as we submit to You. Let this be our desire. In Your name, we pray. Amen.

Respond to Truth

Are you partners or competitors in your marriage?

Have you settled into the dangerous rut of taking each other for granted?

Are you helping each other to grow more spiritual through prayer and through encouragement? Are you focused on your partner's external looks and behavior, or on their eternal direction (1 Peter 3:1–4)?

Are your responses leading your husband to be more and more artificial, or more and more real? (See 1 Peter 3:7.) Do you seek, every day, to understand each other better? How can you practice becoming more and more sensitive to your husband's feelings and ideas?

Are you praying as a couple? Are you watching for God's answers?

Are you becoming more and more spiritually enriched because of your marriage? Or is the way you're treating each other robbing your marriage of God's blessings?

Index